A.I. SURVIVAL GUIDE

A.I. Survival Guide

Artificial Intelligence Basics

CARA CUSACK

Martin Cusack

CaraCusackBooks.com

CONTENTS

| 1 |

Introduction

One crisp morning in November, when the rest of the world was still sipping their coffee, a tremor went through the technological world. An order had been issued from the highest levels of OpenAI. Release a chatbot, and do it fast.

Soon after, the world met ChatGPT, and then everything began to change.

In the past, artificial intelligence was something you'd find in the exclusive realms of top-notch labs and tech giants. Now, it is becoming a household presence. With social media providing wind for its sails, ChatGPT expanded into the world at breakneck speed, surprising even its creators. With its well-spoken language and versatile abilities, it's not just for tech wizards and gurus anymore. It's for everyday programmers, app developers, poets, artists, writers. It is out there for everyone and anyone willing to understand the value it holds. The AI revolution is no longer a dream in some distant future. It just waltzed outside and expanded like the universe itself, with every passing second revealing new stars, new possibilities, and new horizons. It has arrived and is accessible to everyone, anywhere.

I remember the time when news of Microsoft's Tay hit the headlines, a nascent AI chatbot that, in less than 24 hours post-release, spiraled into a whirlpool of offensive, racist messages. Or when Facebook, attempting to jump on the AI bandwagon, found itself grappling with bots inciting hate speech and disturbing content. Each failed attempt was like a scar, serving as a harsh reminder of the perils of uncontrolled AI, and ultimately, led to their withdrawal.

But the narrative began to change with the emergence of Chat-GPT. The bot emerged from the ashes of its predecessors, equipped with the lessons learned from past failures. OpenAI had given this new entrant a lifeline, one that was woven with extensive safeguards and a conscious effort to neutralize biases.

OpenAI's vision didn't stop there. The organization's CEO, Sam Altman, believed in personalized AI chatbots. He envisioned a world where each user could tailor their AI's behavior. Some might opt for a family-friendly version, while others might prefer a more adventurous model. OpenAI pivoted away from the one-size-fits-all approach, creating a new blueprint for public AI.

With this release, a new era of opportunities dawned, but it was an era shadowed by new concerns. Misinformation, privacy breaches, and ethical dilemmas sprang up from the same source that promised unprecedented progress. It was clear that the world needed to understand this new force, now that it was within everyone's reach.

This is where my journey with this AI Survival Guide began. I found myself asking, "How did we get here? How is AI reshaping our lives and our futures?" I realized that the basics of AI weren't just for those in Silicon Valley anymore, they were for everyone. If AI was going to be part of our lives, our work, our conversations, we all needed to understand it.

In this guide, you will find a road map to navigate the world of AI. I will take you through its history, its impact, and its potential. I'll show you its light, the astonishing possibilities for our planet and our society, but also its shadows, the ethical dilemmas, and the risks of misuse.

We're on the threshold of an era, an era where AI isn't just about ChatGPT, but about what comes next. It's an era where AI conversations aren't reserved for the technical experts anymore but for all of us. It's an era that we need to prepare for.

So, here's the AI Survival Guide, a companion for the road ahead. Let's embark on this journey into the brave new world of AI together.

| 2 |

The Dawn of AI

If you ask people when AI began, most will tell you that it started in the last few years or even more recently with the public launch of OpenAI's ChatGPT. The answer might surprise you. Its true timeline is much more fascinating.

The real story actually begins in a bygone era. It was in 1956 that the Suez Crisis unfolded when Egypt nationalized the Suez Canal, leading to military intervention by the British, French, and Israeli forces. The Hungarian Revolution also took place in 1956, with Hungarians rising up against the Soviet-backed government, seeking political freedom and independence. The year also marked the rise of Elvis Presley as a cultural icon, with his groundbreaking performances on television propelling rock 'n' roll into the mainstream. The Civil Rights Movement gained momentum in the United States, spurred by events like the Montgomery Bus Boycott. It was also the year that Dartmouth College was hosting an extraordinary summer conference where the world first heard of the term "Artificial Intelligence". These events and others in 1956 shaped history and left a lasting impact on politics, culture, and social movements.

It was at this Dartmouth College summer conference when John McCarthy, Marvin Minsky, Allen Newell, and Herbert Simon, among others, first introduced the world to the audacious concept of AI. This ignited the imagination and promised a future where machines could replicate human cognition. Little did they know, this term would become the harbinger of a new epoch in human history.

The pioneers of AI were larger-than-life characters in their own right. John McCarthy, often hailed as the "father of AI," not only coined the term "Artificial Intelligence" but also made significant contributions to the field, including the development of Lisp, a high-level programming language used in AI research. Interestingly, McCarthy was a staunch believer in the potential of AI, predicting that "in a generation... the problem of creating 'artificial intelligence' will substantially be solved."

Marvin Minsky, another visionary, was a pioneer of cognitive and AI research. He co-founded the MIT Media Lab and authored seminal works like "Perceptrons," which explored artificial neural networks. Fun fact: Minsky also designed and built the first head-mounted graphical display, a precursor to today's virtual reality headsets.

Meanwhile, Allen Newell and Herbert Simon were trailblazers in exploring how computers could be used to simulate human decision-making processes. They developed the Logic Theorist and the General Problem Solver, programs that could solve complex problems, marking significant milestones in AI's early years. The early years of AI, often referred to as the golden years, were filled with optimism. These early successes sparked a wave of excitement, hinting at the tremendous potential of AI.

This concept of artificial intelligence proposed the idea that machines could be made to mimic human intelligence. They envisioned a future where machines would not only perform calculations but make decisions, learn from experience, and understand natural language. But as with all great endeavors, it was easier said than done.

Thus began the "AI Winter," a period of disillusionment and dwindling investment when AI couldn't live up to its hype. This period was characterized by skepticism and reduced funding. The grand promises of AI had not been realized within the anticipated timelines. The problem-solving machines lacked common sense and understanding of the context. They were excellent problem solvers within a defined framework but struggled when it came to thinking like humans.

However, the relentless spirit of human ingenuity didn't let this dream fade away. The advent of the 21st century brought with it renewed vigor in AI research, propelled by the explosion of big data, advancements in computational power, and machine learning, which revolutionized the landscape of AI. The exponential increase in computational power and the availability of large data sets became the lifeblood of AI algorithms.

Machines were no longer bound by the limits of explicit programming. Instead, they could learn from experience and refine their performance over time, akin to human learning. The emergence of machine learning was a game-changer. Instead of programming machines to solve every possible problem, machines were now able to learn from data and improve their performance. The creation of groundbreaking algorithms, such as backpropagation for training neural networks, revolutionized the field.

Picture a complex, sprawling city, humming with life and energy. This is the neural network, the metropolis of deep learning. In this urban landscape, the algorithm of backpropagation operates like the city planner, overseeing the essential connections and routes that keep the metropolis functioning and evolving. Its key task? To fine-tune the thoroughfares and intersections, the weights between neurons, bringing the city's operations in line with the desired outcome.

Every moment, every event in this vibrant city corresponds to a neuron firing up, data streaming in and flowing through the many layers of the network. Think of it as rush hour traffic, every vehicle carrying a piece of information, converging onto highways, taking exits, and passing through intersections, modulated by weights and directed by activation functions until they reach their final destination, the output.

But then comes the reality check, the city-wide assessment. The output is compared with the desired outcome, revealing an error, the mismatch between the city's current state and the ideal. It's akin to measuring the gap between the traffic flow and the city's master plan.

This is where backpropagation takes center stage again, acting like the diligent city planner conducting a retrospective review. It traces back the traffic and evaluates each route, intersection, and bottleneck, calculating the gradients, and the extent to which each weight contributes to the total error.

Armed with this newfound understanding, backpropagation swings into action, adjusting the city's infrastructure, and the weights of the connections to improve the traffic flow. The learning rate, akin to the city's budget constraints, moderates these changes, not to overhaul the system but to guide it gently towards efficiency.

This process of traffic analysis, feedback, and infrastructure modification repeats in a virtuous cycle. Iteration after iteration, the city continues to evolve and improve, until it reaches a satisfactory state of operation.

This perpetual engine of refinement, powered by backpropagation, has steered deep learning models to unprecedented heights. The algorithm enables these neural metropolises to learn from vast data sets and unravel complex patterns. By fine-tuning their routes and connections, these neural networks learn to make accurate predictions, categorize new data, and function with incredible precision.

Thanks to backpropagation, deep learning models have advanced in leaps and bounds, transforming neural networks into powerful and efficient engines of learning. This algorithm has empowered AI to interpret complex data, recognize intricate patterns, and spawn innovations that are redefining industries.

At its core, backpropagation is the invisible hand that shapes and guides the growth of these neural cities. Its influence, though often unseen, is monumental, driving the growth of AI and defining the course of our future.

Whether it's the diagnostic prowess in healthcare, the recommendation algorithms in online platforms, the self-driving tech in transportation, or the creative abilities in art, AI technologies are becoming an inseparable part of our world.

The term "ChatGPT" began to appear everywhere in late 2022, becoming a new household name. It was the brainchild of OpenAI, an organization at the forefront of artificial intelligence research, known for developing complex language models. Born in the winter chill of 2015, OpenAI held a noble ambition, to ensure that artificial general intelligence (AGI) serves all of humanity, with no exceptions.

Their crowning achievement, ChatGPT, emerged as a conversation-maker. It was built upon a foundation called GPT (Generative Pre-trained Transformer) and made its debut in June 2020 as a research preview. The idea was simple yet ambitious: to introduce ChatGPT to users, let them test its skills, and gather feedback. The AI was designed to be a jack-of-all-trades, assisting with tasks ranging from drafting emails and writing code to answering questions and engaging in general chit-chat.

OpenAI wasn't content to just sit back, though. Every piece of user feedback became a stepping-stone, each interaction a pathway to improving ChatGPT. OpenAI used these insights to keep refining the system, making it smarter and more capable.

Fast-forward to November 2022, a critical milestone in OpenAI's journey. The day had come for ChatGPT to step out of the shadows of the research lab and into the public limelight. It was OpenAI's big step towards making artificial intelligence accessible to all. Now, anyone and everyone can chat with an AI, unlocking endless possibilities across all sectors.

There was, however, a caveat. ChatGPT's knowledge was frozen as of September 2021. It wasn't a limitation, but rather a transparent move to manage user expectations. It encouraged users to seek the latest information for any events or developments beyond that point.

Nevertheless, ChatGPT wasn't stuck in the past. Thanks to the OpenAI API (Application Programming Interface), a link between ChatGPT and the ever-changing internet, the AI stayed relevant. This tool allowed developers to embed GPT-3's power into their own applications, enabling ChatGPT to browse the web and gather up-to-date information, keeping it connected to the world's constant flow of data.

OpenAI's introduction of an open-source "retrieval" plugin allowed developers to enhance their applications with the power of ChatGPT. Plugins are specially devised instruments intended for language models, with a prime focus on safety, and they assist ChatGPT in procuring the most current data, performing calculations, or utilizing services from third parties. This also allows companies to maintain control over their data and address concerns about unauthorized use of their training data.

To enable internet access, OpenAI uses a text-based web browser and the Bing API, which is a search engine API. This combination allows ChatGPT to navigate websites and retrieve relevant information. OpenAI has implemented safety measures to ensure reliable and appropriate information is obtained, as the internet contains unfiltered content that may be less reliable than the training data.

The dawn of AI has been a journey of peaks and valleys, a testament to human ingenuity and perseverance. From the first dreams of intelligent machines to the advanced AI systems of today, we have come a long way. But the story is just beginning, and as we continue our journey, we must ensure that this powerful technology is developed and used responsibly and ethically. Now we have to ensure that we aren't just passive spectators but active participants in shaping the narrative of AI.

And indeed, shaping the narrative we are. We're no longer just dreaming of AI, we're living it. Concepts that once seemed purely the domain of science fiction, such as virtual assistants and autonomous vehicles, are now parts of our everyday reality. Every time we ask Siri a question, recommend a movie on Netflix, or follow a GPS-suggested route, we're interacting with AI.

The same technology that was once looked upon with skepticism now aids in diagnosing diseases, predicting weather patterns, improving crop yields, and even exploring distant planets. But AI isn't solely about impressive technological feats, it also embodies a profound shift in how we understand and interact with the world around us.

The progression of AI isn't simply a linear trajectory of technological advancements. The successes we enjoy today are built upon the foundations laid by the pioneers of the past and shaped by the complex interplay of countless different factors. Scientific breakthroughs, philosophical debates, economic forces, and societal shifts have all played vital roles in shaping the path of AI development.

While we marvel at and even fear these technological advancements, we must also grapple with the ethical and societal questions they raise. As AI's influence continues to grow, we need to consider how to ensure its development and application align with our values and ideals.

How can we ensure AI respects our privacy? What does accountability look like in an age of autonomous systems? Can AI systems ever truly understand or replicate human emotions? These questions aren't just philosophical musings, they're pressing concerns that require thoughtful and deliberate action.

As we stand on the cusp of an AI revolution, the history of AI serves as a stark reminder of the importance of ethical considerations. It challenges us to not only celebrate the technological wonders of AI but also to engage in critical discourse about its implications. From its dawn to its current state, the journey of AI is a testament to human tenacity and innovation, but also a prompt to tread the future path with foresight and responsibility.

| 3 |

It's Just Math

In general terms, AI can be seen as the application of mathematical principles and algorithms to solve complex problems and mimic intelligent behavior. There is no secret sauce involved in AI other than the arrangement of the math to mimic how we humans process data.

Perceptrons are a simple mathematical model of a neuron. Picture AI as a math student. In this world, a perceptron is like a mathematical wizard that imitates a neuron, a cell in our brain. You can think of it as a tiny oracle, processing information and making 'yes' or 'no' predictions.

Like our senses picking up sounds, smells, and sights, the perceptron gathers multiple inputs. These inputs can be seen as various characteristics of an object, such as its length, width, or color. The perceptron assigns a weight to each input, deciding its significance in the final prediction.

Imagine you're baking a cake. Some ingredients are more important than others. A perceptron's decision-making works in much the same way, some factors weigh more than others. Next, our mathematical student adds up all the weighted inputs. It's like tallying the total cost of our cake ingredients, keeping in mind the quantity of each.

After all of these calculations are made, the perceptron uses what's called an activation function, which works like a gatekeeper deciding whether the perceptron should respond 'yes' or 'no.' If the total exceeds a certain value, the gate opens, otherwise, it stays shut. During its training phase, the perceptron learns like a student studying for an exam. It tweaks the weights based on its mistakes to ensure it makes more accurate predictions in the future.

This perceptron is a fundamental unit of more intricate structures called neural networks, a tangled web of interconnected perceptrons. This web, with all its interconnections, allows the network to tackle trickier problems, such as recognizing an object in an image or comprehending human language.

In a nutshell, a perceptron is like a miniature mathematical brain that processes information, assigns importance to various factors, and then, based on these factors, makes a prediction. It's a key player in the world of artificial neural networks, helping AI to classify data or make predictions.

That is the base that makes up the foundation for AI, but mathematics goes even deeper into the workings of AI, allowing it to carry out intricate calculations.

Now, imagine AI as an artist working with various tools and mediums, each serving a unique purpose. From brushes to color palettes, these tools, much like the mathematics involved in AI, help create a masterpiece.

To begin with, AI needs to sketch out its designs, which involve data representation. It uses mathematical structures, vectors, matrices, and tensors, much like an artist uses graphite pencils, markers, and watercolors. These tools allow AI to skillfully manipulate and work with data, shaping it to its requirements.

Just like an artist chooses a style or technique for a painting, AI makes use of algorithms such as machine learning and deep learning. These algorithms, which resemble mathematical models, learn from patterns and make predictions based on data. They function like a detailed guide or a formula, training the AI to create an accurate rendition of the data it works with.

Every artist aims to perfect their art, just as AI strives to optimize certain goals, like reducing mistakes or maximizing results. These goals are reached using optimization methods, firmly rooted in mathematical theories. These methods act like fine-tuning knobs, helping adjust the AI model parameters for better performance and precision.

Art is often open to interpretation, and similarly, AI deals with uncertainties. It uses probability theory and statistical methods to handle ambiguity, estimate likelihoods, and make informed decisions based on the data it has at hand.

Just as colors form the foundation of a painting, linear algebra is fundamental to AI. It's like the palette of the artist, offering a multitude of shades for efficient computation and operations on high-dimensional data. It provides the underpinning for deep learning and neural network architectures.

Imagine an artist working with different brush strokes to add depth to their art. That's what calculus does for AI. It is used for fine-tuning, gradient-based learning, and training models. Essential elements of calculus, like derivatives and integrals, aid in algorithms that adjust the AI models, aiming to reduce errors and enhance performance.

Concepts from Graph Theory are used like a wireframe in sculpting, forming the base for various AI applications. They help understand complex data relationships, much like a sketch helps visualize the final artwork. They're employed in network analysis, recommendation systems, and natural language processing.

Information Theory is like an artist's understanding of texture and composition. It helps measure and understand the amount of information contained in data. Concepts such as entropy and data compression are crucial for handling information in AI systems, just as texture and composition are essential in creating an art piece.

Overall, AI systems rely on mathematical principles, algorithms, and techniques to process data, learn from patterns, optimize performance, and make intelligent decisions. Mathematics provides the foundation for understanding and developing AI algorithms and models, enabling the creation of intelligent systems capable of tasks ranging from image recognition to natural language processing.

| 4 |

Public Perceptions of AI

Let's take a closer look at how we view AI, the same way you might observe a captivating piece of modern art in a gallery. As technology grows, the way we perceive and interact with it is as varied as our individual tastes and interpretations of art.

For some, AI is an exhilarating glimpse into the future, much like an avant-garde masterpiece that pushes the boundaries of creativity. They see it as the always-ready helper, the navigator guiding us through uncharted territories, the uncanny recommendation wizard, or even the revolutionary tool diagnosing complex health issues. These are the optimists in the gallery, the ones who appreciate the potential of AI to transcend our limitations and address our most daunting problems - be it business processes, environmental crises, or health worries.

On the other side of the spectrum, some view AI through a more skeptical lens. For them, AI is an enigma, as unsettling as a looming shadow in the dark. It's the unpredictable factor affecting their job stability, the cold, emotionless customer service bot, the opaque algorithm determining their creditworthiness, or the unseen overseer tracking their digital footprint. These are the people for whom

AI is a harbinger of doom, raising concerns about privacy, job security, and personal freedom.

Our collective perceptions of AI are sculpted to a significant degree by media and popular culture, much like how art trends are influenced by critics and popular media. Hollywood, for instance, has stoked our curiosity and apprehensions about AI with films like "Ex Machina," "Mother,", "The Terminator", "Wall-E," "Bicentennial Man" and "The Matrix" series. In these narratives, AI often oscillates between a helpful companion and an unbridled threat to humanity. While entertaining, these portrayals often project a skewed or hyperbolic image of AI, amplifying existing anxieties and misunderstandings.

Simultaneously, news reports about AI advancements, job losses due to automation, or data leaks facilitated by AI can sway public opinion. The framing and delivery of these stories can either fuel fear or foster a sense of understanding and acceptance, much like a movie review can influence our perception and understanding of it. In the end, we're all observers in the gallery, interpreting AI through our own unique lenses.

Imagine standing at the edge of a cliff looking out at a seemingly infinite ocean, vast and uncharted. For many, AI is a similar vista - something they've heard about but can't quite see clearly. This knowledge gap often gives rise to misunderstandings and unease, acting as stumbling blocks on the path to embracing and harnessing its true potential.

People's perceptions of AI act much like a compass, pointing to the direction in which AI's development and application should move. We have to understand and steer through these varied viewpoints responsibly, much like a skilled captain navigating his ship through a storm. Knowledge of public concerns and aspirations can guide key decisions, from shaping policies and educating the masses to developing ethical designs. An informed public ensures that AI evolves in a manner aligned with our collective values, benefiting everyone.

So, what other factors shape public opinion about AI? One major hurdle is the absence of a universally accepted definition of AI. It's like trying to pin down the exact shape of a cloud, it varies depending on who you ask and the viewpoint from which they see it. Different organizations and researchers have their own interpretations and definitions, adding to the complexity.

AI is a field in constant flux, with new methods and algorithms regularly emerging, adding new layers to the landscape. It's like trying to take a snapshot of a river - the scenery is always changing, making a static definition almost impossible.

AI also covers a broad spectrum of technologies and methods, including machine learning, natural language processing, computer vision, and robotics. Think of it as a mosaic made up of various overlapping pieces, making it tricky to define the boundaries and categories within AI.

Finding the right balance between autonomy and human involvement is another challenge. Determining the degree of autonomy AI systems should possess involves grappling with questions of responsibility, accountability, and potential risks associated with relying heavily on automated decision-making.

It's a curious thing, AI. On one hand, it's like a magician, performing tricks that we can't explain. This so-called 'black box' nature can make understanding AI's decisions as hard as decoding a magician's secrets. But, unlike magic, we need to push for transparency in AI. We need it to not just perform tricks, but also to explain them, to make its decision-making process crystal clear.

Defining AI is like trying to catch a butterfly - elusive and constantly moving. You have to take into account its evolving nature, its ethical implications, and the need to strike a balance between autonomy and human involvement.

AI definitely has a lot of potential, but like all good things, it also comes with its share of worries and concerns. Some people justifiably worry that AI will act like a mirror, reflecting the biases and inequalities in the data it's trained on. This would lead to unfair outcomes in areas like hiring and criminal justice. Others fear AI as a weapon, misused for cyberattacks or even literal warfare. Ethical questions spring up when you think about autonomous systems like self-driving cars or military drones. Who takes the blame if something goes wrong? And then, of course, there's the big worry of AI taking over jobs, leading to a surge in unemployment. How do we address these worries? Well, it's a mix of solid regulations, ethical frameworks, and everyone working together to ensure AI is used responsibly and risks are kept in check.

A popular buzzword in the AI world is 'superintelligence,' the idea that AI could outsmart humans. This raises the big 'control problem.' Can we make sure a superintelligent AI still listens to us and respects our values and goals? The public's views on AI often swing between hope and fear due to discussions about this concept.

Sometimes, fears about AI wiping out humanity can feel more like a sci-fi movie plot than a realistic prediction. Sure, the idea of AI outsmarting us and taking control makes for a thrilling storyline, but in reality, there are numerous safeguards in place to stop this from happening. That said, it's important to stay aware of potential risks that could come from misuse of AI.

Building trust with the public is key. This is where explainable AI comes in. Like a clear window, explainable AI lets people see how AI makes its decisions. This is especially important in sectors like healthcare and finance, where AI's decisions can have a big impact on people's lives. By making AI more transparent, we can help people understand and trust it more.

Transparency in AI is a bit like an open book. It lets you see what's really going on. It helps pinpoint and iron out any biases in the data or the algorithms themselves, making sure that AI isn't just copying societal biases. Transparency doesn't just help check for fairness, but it also makes it easier to assess how reliable an AI system is. It's like having a 'why' to go with the 'how,' which is essential for accountability and ethics in AI.

But, getting to that level of transparency needs more than just tech solutions. Sure, we need things like interpretable models and transparent algorithms, but we also need good old-fashioned conversation. The ability to hold AI systems accountable is especially important when it comes to autonomous systems and critical decisions. If we're going to put AI in the driver's seat, we need to know we can trust it and hold it accountable if something goes wrong. We need to have open dialogues and involve a range of stakeholders, from policymakers to everyday people. By considering different viewpoints, we can make sure concerns are taken into account, and AI is developed responsibly and inclusively.

Looking at where these perceptions of AI come from and what they mean can give us valuable insights into how people will react to AI in the future. Will they welcome it with open arms, resist it, or maybe a bit of both? The journey to find out might tell us as much about ourselves as it does about the technology we're trying to wrap our heads around.

| 5 |

Defining AI Ethics

Now that AI has come to play a substantial role in our daily lives. From how we communicate and learn to how we work and play, AI is leaving an indelible imprint on our world. Yet, along with the immense potential of this technology, come important ethical considerations. But what exactly is AI Ethics? How do we define it?

AI Ethics is like the traffic cop of the tech world, much like ethics in the medical and legal fields. It's there to keep an eye on how artificial intelligence, or AI, impacts our lives and our society. The field dives deep into the big moral questions we need to tackle as AI technology becomes a bigger part of our world.

One of the biggest questions is all about fairness. You see, AI systems learn from our human world, and sometimes, they pick up our biases along the way. Imagine an AI helping to pick candidates for a job, but it favors one group of people over another. Or maybe a facial recognition program struggles to identify folks from certain ethnic backgrounds. AI Ethics is there to figure out how to keep things fair.

Then there's the question of privacy. AI is incredibly good at collecting and making sense of tons of personal data. But with that comes questions about privacy, consent, and how data is used and protected. Especially with technologies like facial recognition or predictive policing, there's a lot to think about. Transparency is key here.

As AI systems start making more decisions on their own, we've got to ask ourselves, who's in control? If something goes wrong, who's responsible? What happens if AI becomes superintelligent and outsmarts us? AI Ethics looks at how to keep control and ensure AI is safe and beneficial. It's a balancing act between pushing forward with AI and ensuring we've got ethical checks in place.

AI Ethics also takes a hard look at how AI might change our society and our economy. Will jobs be lost to automation? How will AI change the way we interact with each other? It's all about understanding the bigger picture.

And let's not forget about the complexity of AI. These systems can be really tough to understand. That's why we need AI that can explain its own decisions, to build trust and acceptance.

Then there's this idea of AI Localism, which is all about giving local governments a role in overseeing AI. By promoting ethical AI development and encouraging engineers to make responsible decisions, we can help reduce risks and make sure AI is a positive force in society.

As AI continues to grow, the field of AI Ethics will only become more critical. The discipline guides us in navigating the ethical challenges AI presents, and the aim is not merely to prevent harm. It's about steering AI towards creating a more fair, inclusive, and better world for all, ensuring that we leverage its potential responsibly. AI Ethics asks the hard questions and strives to find the answers that uphold our shared ethical and moral values.

AI is like a sponge, soaking up all the information it's given. But if it's only fed data from a certain group of people, it's going to make decisions favoring that group. It's like a runaway train speeding through a tunnel, moving straight ahead, illuminating only what it directly encounters and leaving everyone else standing on the platform, waiting in the dark. AI Ethics steps in to say, "Hold on, we need to check this train". It's all about making sure everyone's included, from the moment data is collected right through to when AI systems are let loose.

The thing with AI Ethics is, it's always on the move. As AI grows and changes, so too do the ethical questions we need to ask. It's not a one-time chat, but an ongoing conversation that needs to keep up with the speed of AI. And it's not a conversation for just a few - it needs voices from all corners, policymakers, developers, and the public. Only then can we make sure the benefits of AI are shared fairly.

So, AI Ethics isn't just about setting boundaries for AI. It's like a compass guiding us toward the kind of future we want with AI. A future where tech advancements walk hand in hand with our moral and ethical growth. It's about steering AI to benefit everyone, not just a few.

As the use of AI continues to grow, AI Ethics is going to be right there, keeping pace. This field will be our guide through the ethical maze that comes with powerful technology like AI, ensuring we use it in a way that respects our shared values. It's not just about dodging harm, but about driving AI towards a world that's fairer, more inclusive, and better for all.

| 6 |

Consciousness and Morality in AI

Is AI conscious? The simple answer is no, current AI systems are not conscious. Consciousness is a complex cognitive phenomenon associated with self-awareness, subjective experiences, and the ability to introspect. While AI systems can exhibit impressive capabilities in tasks like image recognition, natural language processing, and decision-making, they lack the subjective experiences and self-awareness that define consciousness in humans. AI systems operate based on algorithms and data processing, without an inherent sense of self or subjective awareness. However, the field of AI ethics and philosophy continues to explore the ethical implications and potential future developments related to consciousness in AI.

While AI has come a long way in the last decade, with developments in machine learning and neural networks giving rise to incredibly sophisticated systems. However, as these systems grow more complex and capable, they start edging into the territory that was once the exclusive domain of living beings. Some researchers and experts are exploring the possibility of creating AI systems that exhibit varying degrees of consciousness. This often starts an intriguing debate surrounding consciousness in AI and the moral responsibilities of these potentially sentient beings.

Even if we do manage to create a truly conscious AI, a new host of moral and ethical dilemmas arise. If an AI has consciousness, does it then have rights? What moral responsibilities do we, as creators and users, have towards these AI? If an AI can think, feel, and suffer, then it becomes ethically unacceptable to treat them as mere tools or objects. Should they be considered an object, a subject, or a completely new category? Each designation comes with its own set of legal and moral considerations and responsibilities.

These questions also force us to consider AI's potential moral responsibilities. If an AI is capable of making autonomous decisions that can affect human lives, then it should also bear moral responsibility for its actions. So, how do we ensure that AI adheres to our ethical standards? How can we 'teach' morality to machines? The challenge here is not just technical, but also philosophical and moral.

If we perceive consciousness as information processing and decision-making abilities, some might argue that certain AI systems exhibit a degree of 'consciousness.' However, if the definition of consciousness extends to self-awareness and subjective experience, it suggests we are far from realizing truly conscious AI.

Even as we venture into creating AI that can simulate emotional responses or learn to react in certain ways based on emotional data, we must understand that this is still a simulation. Can AI truly experience emotions, or are they merely imitating patterns without any feeling? This distinction can have profound implications for how we interact with AI and what moral obligations we have toward them.

As we advance in creating potentially conscious and moral AI, we need to consider its long-term effects on our society. How will the proliferation of such AI systems change our social, cultural, and economic structures? Could it lead to unintended consequences?

As we get closer to the possibility of bringing sentient beings into existence, these considerations move beyond theoretical concerns to practical necessities. While this presents a complex and fascinating area of exploration, it forces us to confront our ideas about consciousness, morality, rights, and responsibilities. It also challenges us to ensure that we create and use AI in a way that aligns with our moral values, ensuring a future where AI benefits all of humanity while respecting the rights and dignity of all sentient beings.

| 7 |

Bias and Discrimination in AI

I have compared AI to a mirror, a kind of societal looking glass because it shows us a reflection of our cultures, communities, and, unfortunately, our biases too. As AI technology becomes an ever more prevalent part of our everyday lives, a critical question emerges. How do we test for and handle bias and discrimination that show up in AI systems? To tackle this, we need to understand where these biases come from, what they lead to, and how we can rein them in.

The root of the problem is the data used to train AI systems. AI learns from the information it's given. If that information is skewed, the AI becomes skewed too. Let's say we have an AI system learning facial recognition, but it's mostly shown pictures of light-skinned individuals. When it comes across darker skin tones, it's likely to stumble. The issue here? The training data isn't diverse enough and that leads to discriminatory outcomes.

The fallout from AI bias can be heavy. It can take societal inequalities that already exist and make them even worse, often hurting the already marginalized groups. Take an AI algorithm used for hiring that ends up sidelining certain demographics, it just perpetuates the disparities in employment. Or consider predictive policing AI used in law enforcement that ends up focusing unfairly on specific racial or ethnic groups, leading to unjust surveillance or even wrongful arrests.

AI, in itself, doesn't have a bias or an inclination to discriminate. It's all down to the data it's fed and how it's designed. Once we realize this, we can be proactive about minimizing AI bias. This means ensuring our training data is diverse and representative, and thoroughly testing our systems to spot and fix biases before they're rolled out. It also means bringing a variety of people into the design and decision-making process, so we're looking at the problem from all angles.

Let me give you a few examples.

1. Amazon's Hiring Algorithm
   In 2018, it was reported that Amazon had abandoned an AI-driven hiring tool because it was biased against women. The system was designed to review job applicants' resumes and select top talents. However, because the training data predominantly consisted of resumes submitted by men (reflecting the male dominance in the tech industry), the system taught itself that male candidates were preferable.

2. Google's Photo Labelling Mishap
   In 2015, Google's image recognition system caused an uproar when it incorrectly labeled African American individuals as "gorillas." The incident highlighted how racial bias can seep into AI systems, especially when training datasets lack diversity. It also emphasized the need for more rigorous testing and auditing of AI systems before deployment.

3. Gender Bias in Language Translation Services
   AI-powered translation services like Google Translate have been shown to perpetuate gender biases. For instance, trans-

lating a Turkish sentence (a language with gender-neutral pronouns) into English often results in gender-stereotyped translations. The sentence "O bir doktor," meaning "They are a doctor," might be translated as "He is a doctor," reflecting the stereotype associating men with the medical profession.

4. Facial Recognition Systems and Racial Bias
Studies have revealed that facial recognition systems, like those used by law enforcement agencies, are more likely to misidentify people of color, particularly women. In one high-profile example, the ACLU conducted a test of Amazon's Rekognition system, which falsely matched 28 members of Congress with criminal mugshots, with false matches which disproportionately involved people of color.

5. Predictive Policing and Racial Disparity

Predictive policing tools like PredPol use historical crime data to predict future crime hotspots. However, these tools can amplify existing biases in law enforcement practices, as areas with historically high police activity, often low-income and minority neighborhoods, continue to be targeted, perpetuating a cycle of over-policing in these communities.

This is why we need to establish standards and regulations to govern AI bias. Holding AI developers accountable for the impact of their systems can drive the creation of more equitable AI. Transparency is key too, as it allows users and regulators to scrutinize AI decision-making processes.

Addressing bias and discrimination in AI is not just about ensuring fairness – it's about the kind of society we want to build with AI. It challenges us to use AI as a tool to mitigate human biases instead of perpetuating them, creating a future where AI serves all of humanity impartially and justly.

| 8 |

Privacy Concerns

In the modern digital landscape, personal data has emerged as an invaluable asset. However, the tremors from the Facebook data privacy scandal have challenged our notions of online privacy. Rooted in the inappropriate use of personal data, this controversy sparked global concern and ignited a dialogue about the imperative for more robust privacy regulations.

The exposure of the Facebook data privacy issue emerged in early 2018 when it came to light that Cambridge Analytica, a political consulting firm, had illicitly accessed the personal data of millions of Facebook users. This disturbing revelation emphasized the precariousness of personal data security and raised serious ethical questions about data collection and utilization practices.

It shined a light on how personal data was unethically harvested by third-party applications, often unbeknownst to users. This pilfered information was subsequently manipulated for personalized advertisements, political interference, and other unscrupulous activities. The incident highlighted the potential perils of unrestricted data collection, underscoring the urgent need for greater transparency in our digital interactions.

Adding to the complexity, Facebook was found struggling with data privacy. Critics argued that the social media giant fell short in protecting user information and responded sluggishly to the data breach. The event intensified questions about Facebook's responsibility and its competence in effectively managing and securing personal data.

Yes, the Facebook data privacy scandal does indeed have implications for AI. AI technologies are becoming increasingly integral to data collection, analysis, and decision-making processes. In the Facebook case, third-party apps were able to collect and misuse user data, which stirred concerns about the ethical and security aspects of data collection practices. AI algorithms are deployed to analyze and interpret the vast amounts of data amassed by platforms like Facebook. The scandal underscored the necessity for responsible and ethical AI practices, such as transparent data collection, consent mechanisms, and secure data storage. It also raised compelling questions about AI's role in assuring data privacy and security in the evolving digital era.

As artificial intelligence becomes more sophisticated, the potential benefits are enormous, but so are the risks, particularly regarding privacy. Now let's examine these risks and how we can manage them to reap the benefits of AI while safeguarding our privacy.

We know AI technologies are data-driven. They rely on large amounts of personal information to operate effectively, which they gather from various sources such as social media, search engines, and internet-connected devices. Can we trust AI with our data? How is our information used, and who has access to it?

An AI system might know things about us that we'd rather keep private, from our internet browsing habits to our health information. AI technologies, like facial recognition, can even track us in the real world, not just online. This extensive data collection can lead to a sense of constant surveillance, causing unease, fear, and discomfort.

But it's not just about what AI systems know, it's also about who they tell. Without proper safeguards, our data could fall into the wrong hands. Cyberattacks targeting AI systems could lead to data breaches, potentially exposing sensitive personal information.

To address these issues, we need robust privacy regulations to control how AI systems can collect, use, and share personal data. Developers should adopt "privacy by design" principles, building privacy protections into AI systems from the outset.

AI can also be part of the solution. New technologies like differential privacy and federated learning can help AI systems learn from data without revealing sensitive information. Users should know what data is being collected, how it's being used, and have the power to opt out if they choose.

In the United States, privacy laws currently present a complex and sometimes contradictory landscape. These laws, differing widely in approach and severity, are a mixture of state and federal regulations, leading to a lack of clarity and the potential for conflict.

Certain states have taken the initiative to establish robust privacy laws to better protect their citizens' data. The California Consumer Privacy Act (CCPA), for example, provides comprehensive rules that are sometimes more stringent than those at the federal level. This disparity in strictness contributes to a complicated environment for businesses that operate in multiple states, each with its own set of privacy regulations.

The lack of overarching privacy regulations in the United States also brings national security into focus. In the absence of stringent laws, sensitive data from citizens could potentially be sold or shared with third parties without transparent procedures or sufficient protections. This scenario not only threatens national security but also erodes public trust in the tech industry.

A significant challenge is the general public's limited under-standing of data privacy laws and their personal rights. Many people overlook privacy policies and terms of service, largely due to their complexity or length, leading to a deficiency in informed consent and individual control over personal data. This public lack of aware-ness further compounds the already intricate situation surrounding privacy in the AI age in the United States.

The General Data Protection Regulation (GDPR) implemented by the European Union (EU) presents a unique challenge to AI and data privacy concerns. It aims to protect individuals' privacy rights and regulate the processing of personal data. However, the applica-tion of GDPR in the context of AI has created a few controversies.

GDPR mandates that individuals provide informed consent for the collection and use of their personal data. However, AI systems often rely on complex algorithms, making it challenging to provide transparent explanations of how data is processed, hindering true informed consent.

GDPR also grants individuals the right not to be subjected to automated decision-making, including profiling, which signifi-cantly affects them. AI systems heavily rely on profiling and auto-mated decision-making, leading to potential conflicts with GDPR requirements.

GDPR emphasizes the principles of data minimization and storage limitations, stipulating that personal data should be col-lected and stored only for specific, legitimate purposes. However, AI systems often collect and retain vast amounts of data, making compliance with these principles challenging.

GDPR imposes restrictions on transferring personal data outside the EU, ensuring that adequate privacy protections are in place. AI systems that operate globally may face challenges in complying with these requirements, particularly when dealing with data collected from multiple jurisdictions.

One well-known example is the case of Google. In 2019, Google was fined €50 million by the French Data Protection Authority (CNIL) for violating GDPR regulations. The fine was imposed due to Google's lack of transparency regarding data processing practices and the absence of valid user consent mechanisms.

Privacy in the age of AI is a complex issue, requiring a balance between the benefits of AI and the need to protect personal information. One solution could be the creation of comprehensive personalized datasets. Picture a kind of personal data bank, where each individual holds the key. AI can only gain access with specific permissions to certain information. This way, we might strike a balance, keeping a firm grip on our privacy while still unlocking the potential of AI to better our lives. It's a delicate balance, but in this brave new world of AI, it's one we'll have to learn.

| 9 |

Superintelligence and the Control Problem

The term "superintelligence" refers to a form of AI that surpasses human intelligence in virtually every aspect, from general wisdom to scientific creativity, and social skills. To really understand this, we have to define the concept of superintelligence, the likelihood of its realization, the control problem it poses, and potential solutions.

Let's start with what superintelligence entails. It's not merely about a computer that can outpace humans in specific tasks. Instead, it's about an AI so advanced that it exceeds human capacity in every significant cognitive activity. Superintelligence could solve problems that humans can't even understand, create technologies beyond our comprehension, and shape the future according to its own objectives.

The Singleton Hypothesis is a concept put forward by philosopher and AI researcher Nick Bostrom, a prominent figure in the discussion about existential risks, including those related to AI. It suggests the possibility that the entire future of the universe might be shaped by a single, globally dominant entity. This entity, termed a "singleton," could be a superintelligent AI, a global governance organization, an omnipotent individual, or any other entity with overwhelming power and control.

In the context of AI, a superintelligent AI singleton would be an AI that has achieved such a level of intelligence and capability that it essentially gains control over the future trajectory of Earth-originating life. It would be able to prevent any potential rivals from emerging, securing a global monopoly of power.

The potential implications of the Singleton Hypothesis are significant. For one, the singleton could use its power for good, preventing existential risks, and ensuring a long and valuable future for Earth-originating life. On the other hand, if the singleton's objectives don't align with human values, it could lead to a future that is not beneficial or even harmful to humanity.

Think of yourself as a conductor, orchestrating a symphony. You have a musical score, a grand vision, and everyone in your orchestra, from the violinists to the percussionists, needs to follow your lead to create harmonious music. The crucial element here? Alignment. It's the same with super alignment in AI. The goal is to get the AI system to follow our human script, aligning with our objectives, goals, and values, creating a symphony rather than a cacophony. That's what the concept of super alignment in AI is all about, getting AI to understand and work towards our human objectives, goals, and values.

The term 'super' doesn't mean we're aiming for perfect alignment, but rather an alignment that's above and beyond the basic understanding of human goals. We want AI systems to not only understand what we're aiming for but to also take into account the complexities and nuances of human values. The aim of super alignment is to ensure that as AI systems grow more powerful, continue to work in ways that are safe, beneficial, and in line with human interests.

This concept is especially important when we consider 'superintelligent' AI. If we fail in this, we might end up with a superintelligent AI that pursues objectives we didn't intend, with potentially catastrophic consequences. It's a bit like having an extremely powerful car that doesn't respond to the steering wheel. It could go anywhere and cause all sorts of damage.

So, the idea behind super alignment is to have AI technology that not only understands our goals but is also adaptable, learning, and evolving with us. It's about building AI systems that are responsive to feedback and capable of self-correction, much like how a good movie director might change their approach based on the responses of their audience.

Without it, there's a risk that a superintelligent AI might not value the things we value. For instance, if it were programmed to manufacture as many paper clips as possible, it might convert all available matter, including humans, into paper clips. This is known as the "paperclip maximizer" scenario. It's a simplified example, but it illustrates the potential dangers of an AI that is incredibly intelligent but lacks human-like values and motivations.

Another concern is that superintelligence might arise suddenly, leaving us unprepared. This is known as the "hard takeoff" scenario. In a hard takeoff, AI undergoes rapid self-improvement, leading to superintelligence in a short period. This is where we are now. We need to prepare for this possibility, ensuring safety precautions are in place before superintelligence emerges.

This raises the control problem. If an AI system is more intelligent than us, how can we control it? That's the conundrum we face when we talk about controlling advanced AI systems. However, there are some clever strategies we can use to make sure we stay in control.

One strategy to solve the control problem is aligning the AI's values with human values, using "boxing" methods to limit the AI's actions, and instilling a "stopping rule" that causes the AI to halt if it starts behaving in undesired ways.

Another more complex strategy is known as 'Value Learning.' This approach is like teaching a child the difference between right and wrong. The AI observes and interacts with humans, learning our values and how we behave. The idea here is that the AI would then act according to these learned values, ensuring it doesn't behave in ways that go against what we, as a society, deem acceptable. However, it's not as easy as it sounds. Defining what these 'values' are and translating them into something an AI can understand is a tricky task.

Then there's 'Reward Modeling,' which is a bit like training a pet. The AI performs an action, a human reviews it, and based on whether the action is deemed good or bad, the AI gets feedback. Over time, the AI learns to model its behavior based on this feedback, taking actions that are in line with what humans consider beneficial. The challenge here is making sure the feedback is accurate and consistent, free of biases, and captures the subtle nuances of human preferences.

The emergence and regulation of superintelligence, however, is not a localized issue. It expands beyond the boundaries of individual countries or organizations, becoming a matter of global concern. The international community has a significant role to play in ensuring the responsible development and deployment of superintelligence. Global cooperation, shared research, and cohesive regulation are necessary to prevent an uncontrolled and potentially harmful AI arms race.

Superintelligence presents both extraordinary opportunities and unprecedented challenges and the solution isn't confined solely to the arena of AI research. It may require incorporating insights from various fields, including philosophy, ethics, and cognitive science. This interdisciplinary approach could offer a more holistic strategy to tackle the control problem, emphasizing the profound complexity and paramount importance of this issue. As we move forward, we must tread cautiously and conscientiously, ensuring that the advent of superintelligence is a boon, not a bane, to humanity.

| 10 |

AI and the Ethics of Replication

Among the controversies surrounding AI involves the ethics of replication. Replication involves the potential for AI to replicate or clone human behavior, personality, or even physical likeness.

Artificial intelligence, empowered by cutting-edge advancements in data analysis and digital imaging, has the capacity to construct incredibly precise replications of human characteristics and behaviors. The reach of AI replication extends from digital assistants emulating our writing style to deepfake technology, capable of grafting one's face onto another's body in a video.

The concept of AI replication is fascinating but also rife with ethical dilemmas. The matter of consent stands at the forefront. Is it ethically sound for AI to replicate a person without their explicit agreement? This issue transcends mere physical appearance and gets into our personal data, which includes our likes, dislikes, opinions, and emotions.

Identity also poses a crucial question. If AI can perfectly replicate us, how does this affect our understanding of self and individuality?

How would these digital replicas reflect our identities - would they represent our authentic selves or a merely idealized version? How unsettling would it be to encounter a digital doppelgänger?

Misuse of this technology is another serious concern. In malevolent hands, the replication abilities of AI can be a tool for deception and manipulation. This leads to worrying phenomena like deepfake-fueled misinformation or even identity theft. Recognizing these risks and devising mitigation strategies is critical.

For a long time, fraudulent activities often involved a stranger claiming to be a figure of authority, such as a police officer, urging immediate monetary help to aid a distressed friend or family member. However, federal regulators caution that the evolution of such scams has taken a technological leap. Now, the urgent call for help could seemingly come from the very friend or family member in question, thanks to a scammer employing a digital clone of their voice.

The Federal Trade Commission (FTC) issued a public alert, drawing attention to the increasing prevalence of scams that use artificially cloned voices. Voice cloning, powered by artificial intelligence, represents one of the newer tools in the scammer's toolbox designed to deceive individuals and extract money.

According to the FTC, a scammer can create a convincing voice clone from just a short audio clip of a person's voice, often sourced from content posted online. Consequently, the scammer's call could sound eerily familiar, mimicking the voice of a known individual.

To protect oneself from such scams, the FTC advises skepticism towards requests for money, especially if the caller sounds like a friend or relative and asks for payment via wire transfer, cryptocurrency, or gift cards. In such cases, individuals should disconnect the call and reach out to the person in question directly to validate their claim.

While the FTC couldn't furnish exact figures on the prevalence of voice-cloning scams, it is evident that this is not mere science fiction. There have been notable cases where voice-cloning technology has been used to perpetrate scams, such as a case in 2019 where scammers, impersonating a CEO, demanded $243,000. In another instance in 2020, a Hong Kong bank manager was duped by a voice clone into making substantial transfers.

As the quality of deepfake videos continues to improve and the technology for voice cloning advances, so does the potential for misuse. In the continuous struggle between security measures and fraudsters, new methods to evade identification protocols are always being devised. One such tactic is facial spoofing, also known as face spoofing attacks. In these scams, fraudsters attempt to trick facial recognition systems by presenting a counterfeit face, such as a photograph, a 3D-rendered model, or even a 3D-printed mask. The advent of AI-assisted technology such as deepfakes has amplified these challenges, presenting a significant hurdle for providers of face recognition solutions.

However, as these threats evolve, so do the defenses. Face spoofing detection systems have progressed, incorporating tools like liveness checks to help combat these new risks. These checks can involve a range of tests, such as examining the texture of the face, the density of facial features, and the relationship between these features, to ascertain the authenticity of the face presented. This level of analysis helps in determining whether a face is real or fake.

The implementation of these advanced technologies not only helps safeguard against fraudulent activities but also streamlines the user onboarding process. By increasing confidence in the true identity of their users, service providers can reduce the time spent on verification, leading to a smoother, more efficient user experience. While the landscape of identity fraud continues to evolve, so too will the measures to protect against it. The dynamic nature of this field promises ongoing advancements in both fraudulent tactics and their countermeasures.

The societal and legal implications are another minefield to navigate. Existing legal frameworks are ill-equipped to handle the ethical and legal repercussions of AI replication. To safeguard individual rights in this new era of AI, we'll need fresh policies and regulations.

Legal disputes surrounding AI replication have emerged, indicating a rapidly evolving landscape of technology and intellectual property rights. For instance, a class-action lawsuit was filed against Microsoft, GitHub, and OpenAI, accusing them of copyright law infringement. This was precipitated by their AI system, Copilot, which was found to have used licensed code snippets from public repositories without providing necessary credit. Copilot's training was based on large-scale public code, and its regurgitation of copyrighted sections has triggered this legal action. The case, still in its early stages, is the first class-action lawsuit in the U.S. challenging the training and output of AI systems. Its outcomes could significantly influence the broader realm of AI, where many businesses profit from software trained on copyright-protected data.

In another distinct legal entanglement, three artists, Karla Ortiz, Kelly Mckernan, and Sarah Andersen, launched a civil lawsuit against Stability AI, Midjourney, and DeviantArt in both San Francisco and London. The artists alleged that their artworks were used in the training databases of these companies' AI models without their consent, leading to the production of derivative works. According to the artists, these companies have violated copyright laws, and the Digital Millennium Copyright Act, and are also infringing on the Unfair Competition law. As AI continues to evolve and grow more sophisticated, such legal conflicts underscore the critical need for a comprehensive understanding and development of intellectual property rights in the digital age.

UK's Home Office abandoned an AI tool for visa application processing after a legal challenge over its alleged "racist" algorithm. The tool was accused of being biased against applicants from certain countries.

These lawsuits serve as pioneering instances of how the intersection of AI and copyright law could shape legal and technological landscapes in the future. The outcomes of these cases could establish important precedents, potentially redefining how copyright law applies to AI systems and their training data.

If the courts rule in favor of the plaintiffs, it could necessitate significant changes in how AI is trained. Companies might need to seek explicit permissions or licenses to use copyrighted content for training AI, potentially impacting the pace of AI development. If they are required to avoid using copyrighted data altogether, this could lead to technical challenges in obtaining sufficient and diverse data to effectively train AI systems.

Furthermore, it could stimulate the development of new legal frameworks or adaptations of existing ones to deal with the specific challenges posed by AI. For example, laws might need to clarify who owns the copyright for AI-generated content, especially when the AI's training involves copyrighted material. This could lead to greater legal complexity, especially when AI models are trained on international data, implicating multiple jurisdictions with different copyright laws.

Conversely, if the courts rule in favor of the defendants, this could solidify the practice of using publicly available data for AI training under the banner of 'fair use'. However, it could also exacerbate concerns about data privacy and the misuse of personal or proprietary information.

In either scenario, these cases highlight the need for ongoing dialogues among technologists, legal experts, policymakers, and the public to balance innovation with ethical considerations and individuals' rights. As AI continues to evolve, ensuring that copyright law keeps pace is a vital challenge that society must confront.

Now let's talk about a controversial but exciting use case for AI in the future. AI has the ability to learn and adapt over time, much like a human would, absorbing information and adjusting its responses based on that information. Now, take this concept a step further and imagine AI replicating an individual, embodying their unique quirks, expressions, and memories. That's the tantalizing and somewhat daunting future we're heading towards.

Digital replication is like making a hologram of a person, but instead of just an image, you're replicating their mind, their character. Currently, we have technologies that can mimic certain aspects of a person. AI chatbots that imitate human conversation, software that replicates voices, and even algorithms that can generate new content based on a person's past writings or videos. We're not far off from a future where these technologies could be combined and refined to the point where they could create a convincing, interactive representation of a specific individual.

While this notion of a digital twin sounds thrilling, there are some major ethical speed bumps to consider. Firstly, there's the question of consent. Should we have the right to create a digital twin of a person, particularly after they've passed away, without their explicit permission? Then, there's the issue of accuracy. No matter how advanced an AI gets, can it truly encapsulate a human being's depth and complexity? And perhaps most pertinently, there's the risk of emotional manipulation. In the hands of the unscrupulous, could these digital twins be used to exploit those in grief, offering false comfort in the guise of a departed loved one?

Grief is a deeply personal process, and the introduction of digital replicas could dramatically change how we navigate it. There's also the potential that digital twins could offer solace, providing a comforting presence and a way to 'keep in touch' with the deceased. But could they also hinder our ability to move forward, keeping us stuck in a cycle of grief? How might they alter the way we remember our loved ones? A digital twin could, after all, offer an edited version of the person, one that might over time reshape our real memories.

The implications of this technology are immense. Imagine a future where digital twins are so convincing they're virtually indistinguishable from the original person. Think of the wisdom, expertise, and insights we could preserve, offering future generations a direct line to the past. But it's also a step towards a new kind of immortality, one that exists within the confines of digital space.

| 11 |

Societal Impact

Artificial intelligence is no longer merely a tool. It's an influential actor shaping societal structures. The rise of AI heralds a transformative epoch, a time of immense promise as well as complex challenges. Let's explore the potential societal impacts of AI, which could incite new forms of inequality and social issues, while also creating unprecedented opportunities for societal progression.

As these technologies continue to evolve and mature, their influence on our societies and communities becomes more profound. On the one hand, AI can fuel societal advancement, making our lives more convenient, efficient, and connected. On the other, it might inadvertently create or exacerbate social inequalities and challenges.

The potential for AI to automate numerous job roles is both a boon and a potential source of social discord. While automation can increase productivity and relieve humans from menial tasks, it also raises the concern of job displacement, with consequences that could ripple through society. The challenge lies in managing this transition without marginalizing significant sections of the workforce.

AI is also transforming our societal structures in subtler ways. With its ability to analyze massive data sets and predict behavior, AI can shape the content we consume, the goods we purchase, and even our political views. While this could lead to more personalized experiences, it could also fuel a "filter bubble" effect, where individuals are insulated from contrasting perspectives, which can lead to increased polarization. This phenomenon underlines the criticality of diverse data inputs and unbiased algorithms in AI systems to avoid contributing to societal polarization and the creation of echo chambers.

AI advancements also have the potential to widen existing social disparities, particularly with regard to access to technology. The advent of AI and other advanced technologies could create a digital divide, where individuals with access to these resources reap substantial benefits, while those without such access are left behind.

Yet, AI also holds the promise of social progression. It has the potential to revolutionize sectors like healthcare, education, and environmental management, making these services more efficient and accessible. In addition, AI could enable us to address complex societal challenges, such as climate change and global health crises, in ways that were previously unimaginable.

Artificial intelligence stands at the forefront of societal transformation. Its impact extends beyond the realm of technology, resonating through our societal structures and norms. As we embrace the AI era, we must navigate these opportunities and challenges with care, ensuring that the benefits of AI are broadly shared and its potential pitfalls are mitigated.

In scenarios where AI systems make decisions that impact human lives, such as autonomous vehicles or medical diagnoses, how can we ensure accountability and transparency? How can we build AI systems that respect our ethical norms and values, and who gets to decide what those norms and values are? These are complex, multi-faceted questions that need collaborative efforts from technologists, policymakers, ethicists, and society at large to address.

AI also has the potential to exacerbate existing biases if not carefully managed. As machine learning models are trained on historical data, they could perpetuate and even amplify human biases embedded in that data. This raises important issues of fairness and equity, particularly in areas such as criminal justice, lending, and hiring, where algorithmic decisions could significantly affect individuals' lives.

Yet, for all the promises of AI, a key challenge lies in ensuring equitable access to its benefits. The risk is that these advanced technologies might primarily benefit those who already have access to resources, further exacerbating social inequalities. Hence, there's a need for proactive strategies that ensure AI is used in a manner that benefits society broadly, rather than just a privileged few.

In the coming decades, the societal impact of AI will continue to unfold. As we stand on the cusp of this transformation, it's imperative to foster a thoughtful, inclusive dialogue about the societal implications of AI. This dialogue should guide the development of regulations, public policy, and industry practices, ensuring that we steer AI in a direction that aligns with our collective societal goals and values.

| 12 |

AI, Jobs, and Economic Implications

Artificial Intelligence is rapidly altering the landscape of work and the economy at large. This revolution, often termed the 'fourth industrial revolution', presents a complex narrative filled with promises of increased productivity and threats of job displacement. We are seeing this right now and feeling the effects. While I am editing this chapter, there is an ongoing strike between the Screen Actors Guild, the American Federation of Television and Radio Artists (SAG-AFTRA), and the Alliance of Motion Picture and Television Producers around this very topic. One of the reasons is their desire to use background actors for a day and then create a digital replication of that person to use in perpetuity without payment or consent. This move essentially signals the end of background acting as a viable career path.

The increasing sophistication of AI has enabled it to take over an array of tasks, transforming the nature of jobs in every sector. From manufacturing and logistics to retail and healthcare, AI's capabilities to automate routine tasks are becoming apparent. This change, while promising in terms of increased efficiency and productivity, could displace jobs, especially those involving repetitive tasks.

However, it's not just about job displacement. AI is also creating new jobs and industries. For instance, there's a growing demand for AI specialists who design, develop, and maintain these systems. Additionally, AI's ability to analyze data can uncover new insights, leading to the creation of entirely new business models and services, thus creating jobs that didn't exist before.

The rise of AI is likely to lead to economic shifts, analogous to the shifts caused by previous technological revolutions. In the short term, these changes can cause disruption and uncertainty. For instance, individuals whose jobs are replaced by automation may face economic hardship unless they can transition into new roles.

On a more positive note, AI's impact on the economy can also lead to a significant boost in productivity and economic growth. Automation can lead to cost savings for businesses, which can result in lower prices for consumers and higher profits for companies. Furthermore, AI can help in predicting market trends, making supply chains more efficient, and personalizing customer experiences, all of which can stimulate economic growth.

AI's influence on jobs and the economy is undeniably profound, transforming the way we work and live. This transformation holds potential for economic growth and prosperity, but it also presents challenges that need careful handling.

Jobs That Could Be Replaced:

Manufacturing Workers: Automated machines and robots, enhanced by AI, can perform tasks such as assembling products, quality control, packaging, and shipping more efficiently than humans and without breaks.

Drivers: With the advent of autonomous vehicles, roles like truck drivers, taxi drivers, and delivery drivers could potentially become obsolete. We are already seeing autonomous delivery vehicles in food and grocery delivery. As these technologies continue to improve and gain wider acceptance, we may witness a transition where delivery services move increasingly from human-operated to AI-driven, potentially necessitating the need for drivers to upskill or transition into different roles.

Farm Laborers: Farm laborers, who are typically responsible for manual, repetitive tasks such as planting, watering, and harvesting, could be replaced as AI-powered machinery and robotics become increasingly capable. This technology can perform these tasks more efficiently and without fatigue, potentially making human labor redundant in many agricultural operations. AI-driven vehicles can eliminate weeds from crops faster and more accurately than humans.

Retail Cashiers: Automated checkout systems and self-service kiosks are increasingly replacing human cashiers in grocery stores, fast food chains, and other retail outlets. Amazon Go stores operate through the use of sensors, advanced AI algorithms, and computer vision technology, enabling it to identify the items a customer picks up and even when these items are placed back on the shelves.

Data Entry Clerks: Machine learning algorithms are getting adept at tasks involving the entry and processing of data, posing a real threat to jobs that involve manual data entry.

Customer Service Representatives: AI-powered chatbots and virtual assistants can answer customer queries 24/7 and are becoming more sophisticated in understanding and responding to complex requests.

Human Language Translators: The demand for human language translators could potentially diminish as AI-based translation tools become more accurate and nuanced in their understanding of languages. These AI systems, powered by sophisticated machine learning models, are capable of learning the complexities of human languages, including slang, cultural nuances, and idioms, thereby increasingly performing translations in real-time with high precision.

New Jobs That AI Could Create:

AI Specialists: This includes roles such as AI engineers, AI ethicists, and data scientists who will design, develop, and ensure the responsible use of AI systems.

AI Trainers: AI trainers are professionals who guide the learning of artificial intelligence systems by providing them with appropriate data, refining their performance, and helping them better understand and interact with the world, thereby playing a pivotal role in the development and improvement of these systems.

AI Auditors: AI system outputs will have to be constantly monitored to ensure they are accurate and performing their assigned tasks correctly.

Robot Operators: As autonomous delivery robots gain prominence, there will likely be a surge in demand for robot operators who can remotely monitor and control these machines. This emerging profession not only offers new job opportunities but also requires a unique skill set, blending technological proficiency with logistical oversight.

Data Privacy Experts: As more data gets generated and used by AI systems, the need for professionals who can ensure data privacy and compliance with laws will grow.

Robotics Engineers: The increasing adoption of robots in various industries, including healthcare, manufacturing, and logistics, will spur demand for professionals who can design, maintain, and repair robots.

Personalized Medicine Providers: AI's ability to analyze vast amounts of data can help in providing personalized medical care, leading to roles like genetic counselors who interpret and explain genetic and genomic data.

Renewable Energy Managers: AI can optimize the generation and distribution of renewable energy. This can create jobs for those who can manage these complex systems.

Jobs That Could Transform:

The influence of AI isn't confined to traditional industries. It's also permeating creative fields, including programming, arts, music, and acting, causing significant transformations.

Programmers: With AI algorithms becoming capable of writing and debugging code, some fear that programmers' jobs might be at stake. However, the reality is likely more nuanced. Programmers might find their roles evolving rather than disappearing, as they shift towards more complex tasks such as system design, strategic decision-making, and human-computer interaction.

Artists: AI has been used to create paintings, sculptures, and even digital art, raising questions about the future of human artists. However, the creative process is complex and deeply personal, often tied to human experiences and emotions that AI currently cannot replicate. Therefore, AI may serve as a tool for artists, helping them explore new creative avenues rather than replacing them.

Musicians: AI is increasingly being used to compose music. But like visual art, music is a deeply human endeavor, bound to emotions and experiences. While AI might take over the composition of background scores or elevator music, human musicians will likely always be needed for the soulful, creative aspect of music. They may also find new roles in manipulating and interacting with AI to create novel forms of music.

Actors: Deepfake technology and AI can create realistic images and videos of people, including actors. Yet, acting involves conveying human emotions and experiences convincingly, a feat that AI can't fully achieve yet. Audiences often form emotional attachments to actors, something that is unlikely to be replicated with AI. Still, actors might find AI impacting their profession, perhaps through the rise of virtual characters or the use of AI in pre-production for script analysis and character development.

Writers: AI has been used to generate text, including stories, poems, and news articles. Yet, writing involves not just arranging words in an appealing way, but also conveying human experiences, emotions, and subtleties. It's unlikely that AI will replace human writers entirely. Instead, writers might find AI becoming a helpful tool, assisting with tasks like research, drafting, editing, and perhaps even providing creative inspiration.

It's important to remember that while AI is reshaping these jobs, it's unlikely to replace them entirely. These roles involve a depth of creativity, emotion, and human connection that AI has yet to achieve. However, professionals in these fields should be prepared for transformations in their work as AI becomes an increasingly integral part of their industries.

The emerging AI economy also presents an opportunity for new business models. With the advent of AI-powered services like personalized marketing, predictive maintenance, and financial advisory, companies can deliver innovative, high-value services. This, in turn, could lead to economic expansion and job creation in various sectors.

However, this transformation might also exacerbate economic inequality. The benefits of AI are often reaped by those with access to advanced technology and the skills to leverage it, while those without such access risk falling further behind. This digital divide, if unchecked, could lead to a wider wealth gap and social instability.

The displacement of jobs by AI could also lead to significant social challenges. The transition to new jobs often requires reskilling, which may not be accessible or affordable for all workers. Policy interventions, such as offering affordable education and training opportunities, will be crucial to ensuring a just transition.

In the long term, AI's contribution to economic productivity could be substantial. By automating routine tasks, AI can free up human time for more complex, creative tasks, leading to increased productivity and economic growth. Additionally, AI can lead to cost savings, which can lower consumer prices and increase profits for businesses.

However, the journey to this AI-enabled future is fraught with challenges, from managing job displacement to ensuring fairness in AI systems. We will have to adopt a holistic approach that maximizes the benefits of AI while minimizing its potential pitfalls. By promoting inclusive access to AI technology, fostering lifelong learning and reskilling initiatives, and maintaining a vigilant eye on AI ethics, we can strive for an AI-driven economic future that benefits all.

| 13 |

AI and Human Interaction

AI and its influence on human interactions present both a fascinating exploration into future possibilities and navigation through potential ethical dilemmas. Today, we interact with AI-powered personal assistants such as Siri and Alexa, engage with chatbots on various websites, and are subtly influenced by recommendation algorithms on content streaming platforms and in targeted advertising.

Conversational AI, in particular, has opened avenues for unprecedented human-machine interaction. With the help of natural language processing and machine learning, AI systems can now engage in human-like conversation, mimicking human dialogue for a more organic interaction experience.

The advent of AI-powered social robots has ushered in a new era of companionship, assisting in everyday tasks, providing company, and even offering therapeutic benefits. Yet, these advancements come with their own set of challenges, the potential for human emotional manipulation, privacy concerns, and dependency issues, all of which require careful consideration and regulation.

The influences of AI are particularly noticeable within social networks and online communities. It is here that AI-based algorithms often dictate the content displayed on our feeds, subtly influencing our perceptions and interactions. However, as I said earlier, this very feature can also lead to the creation of 'echo chambers', where individuals are exposed to content reinforcing their pre-existing views and beliefs, limiting exposure to contrasting perspectives.

AI's role isn't limited to crafting efficient tools but also encapsulates understanding and navigating the complexities of human communication, empathy, and ethics. It underscores the importance of ensuring that these technological integrations enhance, not dilute, the richness of human interaction.

AI has already begun enhancing personalized learning experiences. Educational platforms powered by AI provide tailored experiences, taking into account individual learning styles and preferences. Intelligent tutoring systems and adaptive learning algorithms scrutinize student performance to offer focused recommendations, making education a more engaging and effective process.

AI is also transforming the entertainment industry and content creation. Algorithms not only suggest personalized content on streaming platforms but also play a role in creating music, art, and more. The integration of chatbots and virtual assistants in gaming and interactive storytelling is further blurring the lines between reality and virtual worlds, enhancing user experiences significantly.

AI-powered virtual companions have also been instrumental in engaging with different demographics, such as children and seniors. They offer companionship, assist with tasks, and even provide therapeutic benefits to individuals, including children and the elderly. An excellent example is Moxie, a robot designed to help kids learn social, emotional, and cognitive skills through play-based learning. AI chatbots are also revolutionizing mental health care by providing readily available, stigma-free support.

AI is also redefining our interactions in the realm of virtual reality (VR) and augmented reality (AR). These immersive technologies, when combined with AI, can simulate social interactions, teleport us to places we cannot physically visit, and create shared experiences that were previously unimaginable. People can participate in virtual gatherings, visit virtual places of interest, or engage in shared activities, effectively reducing feelings of loneliness and isolation.

Elon Musk's Neuralink presents a compelling exploration of the potential integration of AI with our neural activity. While Neuralink's primary focus is on developing implantable brain-machine interfaces (BMIs), AI could play a crucial role in enhancing the functionality of these BMIs. AI can be employed to analyze neural data, interpret signals, adapt and optimize performance based on individual neural patterns, and even assist in neurorehabilitation.

One of the more interesting applications of AI has been its incorporation into language translation services. Language translators, who for centuries have served as bridges between cultures, now find themselves competing with sophisticated AI models capable of providing near-instant translations. While the human touch in translation, with its nuanced understanding of cultural contexts, remains irreplaceable, the sheer convenience of AI-driven instant translation cannot be ignored. Modern translation tools leverage complex AI algorithms to interpret and translate multiple languages in real time, fostering global communication and bridging linguistic barriers.

Imagine a future where you are in a virtual video meeting like Zoom or Skype with people from other countries speaking multiple different languages. AI-assisted instant translators and voice generators could allow you to hear each person speaking in your native language while they are hearing you in theirs. This not only changes the way we interact with people from different linguistic backgrounds but also reshapes the demand for professional human translators.

Nevertheless, we need to tread with caution. The ethical challenges presented by AI in terms of privacy, data security, and even our perception of what it means to be human, require careful consideration. As AI continues to augment and sometimes replace human interaction, we need to develop them in ways that respect our human values, individuality, and the rich diversity of our social fabric.

AI is more than just a technological revolution. It is an integral part of the evolving narrative of human interaction in the 21st century.

| 14 |

AI and Children

The influence of AI on children's lives presents its own unique set of opportunities and challenges. Artificial intelligence is gradually becoming an integral part of children's lives, shaping their learning, play, and social interactions. The integration of AI into children's lives also introduces them to complex social and ethical issues at a young age. Understanding AI, its benefits, and its limitations is becoming a necessary part of digital literacy for today's children.

AI has the potential to revolutionize education by offering personalized learning experiences. For example, AI-based educational software can adapt to each child's individual learning style and pace, offering customized lessons and feedback. This personalization can enhance learning outcomes, making education more engaging and effective for children.

By analyzing a child's learning patterns and performance, AI can provide a personalized learning path, offering custom-tailored content and pacing for each individual. This approach can greatly enhance learning outcomes and engagement. AI platforms such as DreamBox Learning and Carnegie Learning provide adaptive learning experiences in Math and other subjects, aiding students to master concepts at their own pace.

Smart toys, which often come with voice recognition and conversational capabilities, offer interactive play experiences. While these toys can be engaging and educational, they also raise questions about privacy and data security. As these toys interact with children, they collect vast amounts of sensitive information, raising concerns about how this data is used and who has access to it.

There is also a growing interest in using AI to foster creativity in children. Platforms like Winky Think Logic Puzzles or Google's AI Doodle Game encourage children to solve problems, create art, and even make music, all guided by AI algorithms. These applications not only entertain but also stimulate children's imagination, creativity, and critical thinking skills.

Interactive AI-powered toys and companions, like the robot Moxie, are blurring the lines between play and learning. Moxie uses machine learning to interact with children, assisting them in developing social, emotional, and cognitive skills. Its ability to recognize and respond to the child's behavior, conduct conversations, and even remember past interactions makes it an engaging and adaptive playmate. Yet, its role as a quasi-friend introduces important questions about the emotional bonds that might form between children and AI.

The emotional and social implications of children interacting with AI systems need careful consideration. AI systems lack true emotional understanding or empathy, which are critical for children's development. Therefore, while AI can be a beneficial tool, it is important to balance its use with real human interaction and traditional forms of learning and play. The lack of emotional intelligence in AI systems raises concerns about their suitability as companions or tutors for children.

AI's integration into children's lives also calls for proper education about AI itself. Children need to understand what AI is, how it works, its potential, and its limitations and potential for abuse. This understanding will not only prepare them for a future where AI is ubiquitous but will also teach them to use these technologies responsibly and ethically.

| 15 |

AI in Personalized Learning

Now let's go a little deeper into the applications and potential for personalized learning. AI has emerged as a transformative tool in the education sector. From intelligent tutoring systems to AI-driven educational apps, these technologies are tailoring learning experiences to individual students' needs, enabling personalized learning paths that adapt to each student's pace and style of learning. It enables a shift from the traditional one-size-fits-all teaching approach to a more individualized learning experience. It can analyze a student's learning patterns, detect areas of difficulty, and provide customized content to help overcome these challenges. This personalized attention can potentially lead to more effective learning, fostering a deeper understanding of the subject matter. These innovations are transforming both the teaching and learning processes.

One prime example of this is Carnegie Learning's MATHia. This AI-infused software delivers a personalized approach to math education, adjusting to each student's pace. It provides instant feedback and additional exercises when a student encounters difficulty with a concept, continuously assessing and adapting the content and difficulty level based on the learner's progress.

Another notable AI-based tool is Thinkster Math, which customizes math learning. The platform analyzes various factors, including how a student tackles a problem, the time taken, and the mistakes made. Based on this data, it tailors the learning content, enhancing students' conceptual understanding and problem-solving skills.

Content Technologies Inc.'s Cram101 also employs AI to reform traditional study methods. It simplifies textbooks into smart study guides, breaking down lengthy chapters into easy-to-digest summaries, flashcards, and practice tests. This makes learning more manageable and less overwhelming for students.

Research on AI in personalized learning supports the effectiveness of these methods. A Stanford University study in 2016 indicated that AI-enhanced personalized learning significantly improved student performance and engagement. The study revealed that students using personalized learning platforms scored noticeably higher than their counterparts using conventional learning methods.

Further supporting these findings, research by the Center for Digital Education suggested that AI-facilitated personalized learning could accelerate learning speed by 50%, with improved knowledge retention rates.

The real-world application of AI-enabled personalized learning has yielded promising results. For instance, MATHia's personalized teaching style has led to improved student performance, with schools using MATHia reporting an average growth of 82% on the NWEA MAP Growth math assessment. Similarly, Thinkster Math claims its users see an average improvement of 10-15% in their math scores within the first three months.

AI's role in education goes beyond personalizing learning content. It also has the potential to automate administrative tasks, such as grading assignments and managing schedules, thereby freeing up time for educators to engage more deeply with their students.

Could AI replace teachers? The answer is no, AI is more likely to augment teachers' capabilities by providing personalized learning tools and data-driven insights, rather than replacing them, as the human element in teaching and mentoring is irreplaceable.

AI can pinpoint knowledge gaps and provide targeted exercises to address gaps in knowledge and understanding. It also provides real-time feedback, enabling students to identify and rectify their mistakes immediately. It can also track a student's learning journey, supplying invaluable data to educators to further optimize the learning experience. These advancements contribute to a more efficient and effective education system.

| 16 |

AI and Seniors

Seniors face a myriad of critical issues such as loneliness and healthcare management where AI has the potential to vastly improve the quality of life while enhancing their ability to live independently. As technologies continue to evolve, they are creating innovative solutions tailored to the unique needs and challenges of seniors.

AI-powered virtual companions are playing an increasingly important role in alleviating loneliness and fostering emotional well-being among seniors. These companions, such as the ElliQ by Intuition Robotics, engage seniors in meaningful conversation, play games, offer cognitive stimulation, and provide companionship, reducing feelings of isolation. They use machine learning to understand the user's preferences and patterns, enabling them to offer personalized interactions and support.

It also opens new horizons for social engagement through social media platforms and online communities. With the aid of AI algorithms, social media platforms can suggest relevant content, interest groups, and connections based on a senior's preferences and habits, encouraging active engagement. Online communities specifically designed for seniors offer a platform for shared interests, discussions, and connections, fostering a sense of belonging and community.

AI's role in healthcare is rapidly expanding, offering significant benefits for seniors. Telehealth services facilitated by AI enable seniors to connect with healthcare professionals remotely, providing an essential healthcare access point for those with mobility issues. It can also assist with regular remote monitoring of vital health parameters, enabling timely intervention if anomalies are detected. AI-powered systems can send reminders for medication and appointments, contributing to improved health management.

In terms of daily living, AI-powered smart home assistants, like Amazon's Alexa or Google Home, can provide seniors with companionship, entertainment, and assistance with routine tasks. From setting reminders and providing news updates to controlling home automation systems for lighting, heating, or security, these assistants enhance seniors' ability to live independently.

Virtual Reality (VR) and Augmented Reality (AR) technologies, combined with AI, can offer seniors immersive experiences that simulate social interactions and environments. For instance, they can participate in virtual gatherings, explore places of interest, or engage in virtual activities, all from the comfort of their home. This not only provides entertainment but can also help reduce those feelings of loneliness and isolation.

AI can also provide invaluable support to seniors suffering from Alzheimer's or other forms of dementia. GPS-based tracking systems can alert caregivers if the senior wanders off or gets lost, ensuring their safety. AI-powered applications can provide cognitive exercises individually tailored to their capabilities, helping to slow cognitive decline and providing mental stimulation.

AI can also play a pivotal role in safeguarding seniors from scams, which they are often disproportionately targeted by. AI-powered fraud detection systems can monitor seniors' online activities and financial transactions to identify and alert them of potential scams. For instance, these systems can detect unusual transaction patterns, warn about suspicious emails or phone numbers, and even identify phishing websites that mimic trusted organizations. By providing real-time alerts, these systems can prevent seniors from falling prey to scams and financial fraud.

In addition, AI can also aid in detecting robocalls, one of the common mediums for executing scams. By analyzing the calling pattern, frequency, and origin, AI can identify potential robocalls and block them before they reach the intended recipient. Advanced systems can even mimic human conversation to engage the robocall, keeping it occupied and preventing it from targeting others.

Another important application of AI for seniors is fall detection and emergency response. With AI technology, wearable devices or home systems can identify when a senior has fallen and automatically alert designated contacts or emergency services. For example, Apple's Watch Series 4 and later models incorporate fall detection, sending an alert to the wearer when a hard fall is detected. If the wearer doesn't respond within a specific time frame, the watch can automatically call emergency services.

AI can also assist in the management of mental health for seniors. By detecting changes in speech patterns, activity levels, or online interactions, AI tools could identify symptoms of stroke, depression, or anxiety, prompting early intervention. Mental health chatbots, such as Woebot, use AI to provide cognitive behavioral therapy techniques, offering immediate psychological support and coping mechanisms.

In terms of independence, AI has the potential to extend the time that seniors can live independently. Besides automated systems that manage home security, lighting, and temperature, technology can enhance the safety and comfort of seniors in their homes. For instance, AI-powered wheelchairs or mobility scooters can navigate environments independently, enabling seniors with mobility issues to move around with ease.

Again, it is important to note that AI systems designed to assist seniors should always prioritize privacy and consent. Seniors should have a clear understanding of what data is being collected, and how it's being used, and should have the option to opt out if desired. With the right balance of technology and privacy, AI can provide a critical layer of protection for seniors.

While AI offers substantial potential benefits, we have to discuss the balance of technology with real-life social connections. AI can complement, but not replace, the richness of human interaction. An optimal approach to addressing loneliness and improving the quality of life for seniors would incorporate AI solutions alongside genuine human companionship and care.

Overall, while AI presents a wealth of opportunities to improve the lives of seniors, its successful integration relies on accessibility and usability. User-friendly design, clear instructions, and ongoing support are crucial to ensure that seniors can effectively use and benefit from AI technologies. As the senior population continues to grow, the thoughtful application of AI in senior care has the potential to make significant strides in enhancing the quality of life, health outcomes, and independence.

| 17 |

AI in Scientific Discovery

AI is making remarkable progress in scientific exploration and discovery. It expedites processes, identifies intricate patterns, and constructs novel hypotheses, thereby pushing the boundaries of human understanding. It has proven itself as a revolutionary tool that is transforming scientific discovery across a broad spectrum of fields. By leveraging machine learning, data analysis, and pattern recognition, AI provides unmatched capabilities to delve into uncharted territories and decipher complex scientific phenomena.

AI operates as a potent fount of inspiration, augmenting human creativity and imagination. By exploring vast datasets and generating intriguing ideas, AI systems can inspire scientists to embark on new research paths and make innovative connections.

As a computational microscope, AI is equipping scientists with the ability to gain insights into entities, processes, and phenomena that would otherwise be out of reach. By processing vast amounts of data, AI algorithms can glean new understanding and facilitate discoveries that were previously beyond the grasp of traditional experimental approaches. Its ability to process colossal amounts of data significantly exceeds that of humans. It can discern minute correlations and complex patterns that might otherwise be overlooked. This ability empowers scientists to glean insights from big data sets across various disciplines, including genetics, climate science, and astronomy. As a result, AI has become an invaluable tool for many researchers.

The growing dependence on AI in research may also impact the scientific community. It could alter the skill sets needed for scientific research, placing greater emphasis on computational skills. This change could potentially widen the gap between institutions with sufficient resources to procure cutting-edge AI systems and those without such resources.

Despite these challenges, the infusion of AI into scientific discovery presents tremendous potential. However, it is vital to address these ethical considerations to ensure a balanced and inclusive scientific future. As we welcome this new phase of AI-driven research, we must constantly assess and adapt to the ethical challenges it presents.

AI has had a fundamental role in astrophysics, assisting scientists in decoding the cosmos. These algorithms have enabled the discovery and classification of cosmic bodies, such as galaxies, black holes, and exoplanets. By analyzing astronomical data gathered from telescopes and observatories, AI algorithms can spot subtle patterns and anomalies, leading to breakthroughs in our understanding of the universe's structure, evolution, and even the nature of dark matter.

In genomics, AI has fundamentally transformed our capacity to analyze and interpret massive volumes of genetic data. The algorithms can detect patterns within DNA sequences, predict gene functions, and identify genetic markers linked to diseases. This has quickened the discovery of potential drug targets, personalized medicine, and advancements in gene editing techniques.

AI has had a substantial impact on materials science by expediting the discovery of new compounds and materials with desirable properties. There have been significant strides in the development of advanced materials across various domains.

For instance, in energy storage, AI has accelerated the discovery of new materials for systems like batteries, by harnessing large datasets and conducting simulations to pinpoint promising material candidates exhibiting superior energy density, stability, and charging or discharging efficiency.

In catalysis, AI has streamlined the optimization of catalyst materials essential for chemical reactions. It accomplishes this by modeling and simulating a variety of catalyst structures and reaction conditions, allowing for the prediction of the most effective catalysts and fostering more efficient and sustainable chemical processes.

In the electronics sector, AI has enhanced the discovery of novel materials with desirable properties, which in turn, promotes the development of advanced and efficient electronic devices. This is achieved through AI algorithms that speed up the search for materials possessing high conductivity, improved thermal stability, and enhanced optical properties.

In photovoltaics, AI algorithms analyze and predict the performance of various material combinations, which aids researchers in identifying materials with superior light absorption, charge transport, and stability. This results in more efficient and cost-effective solar cells.

In the broader arena of materials discovery, AI has expedited the process by analyzing voluminous data and executing virtual simulations, which facilitates the identification of new materials with specific properties such as increased strength, flexibility, or conductivity, suitable for a vast range of applications.

The pharmaceutical industry has also been revolutionized by optimizing the process of drug discovery and development. It can process vast volumes of chemical data, predict molecular properties, and identify potential drug candidates. This capability is especially beneficial in fields like drug discovery, where AI can anticipate the efficacy of potential drugs, saving researchers substantial time and effort. It has also been leveraged to repurpose existing drugs for new medical applications. By processing large-scale biomedical datasets, AI can identify potential new uses for drugs beyond their original intended applications. This approach has shown potential in quickly identifying treatments for rare diseases, reducing the time and cost associated with traditional drug development. This speeds up the identification of promising therapeutic compounds, reducing the time and cost associated with traditional drug development processes.

Climate science usage of AI has played a huge role in analyzing data from various sources, including satellite imagery, weather stations, and climate models. It can detect patterns, predict climate change impacts, and optimize climate models. This assists scientists in better understanding the Earth's climate system, predicting extreme weather events, and formulating strategies for climate adaptation and mitigation.

Quantum physics is utilizing AI to help decode the complexities of quantum systems. Using machine learning algorithms, researchers can predict and simulate the behavior of quantum systems, contributing to the development of quantum computing and communication technologies. These advancements may usher in a new era of computational power and security, which could have significant implications across many fields, from cryptography to drug discovery.

In the area of ecology, AI is enhancing species identification and biodiversity monitoring. AI-powered image recognition algorithms can process photos from field studies or citizen science projects, accurately identifying and cataloging species. This not only accelerates the processing of ecological data but also provides insights into species distributions, populations, and behaviors. These advancements are critical for conservation efforts and understanding ecological dynamics.

AI is revolutionizing oceanographic research through the use of autonomous underwater vehicles (AUVs). Equipped with AI systems, these AUVs can collect oceanographic data, monitor marine ecosystems, and even detect underwater archaeological sites. These AI-powered technologies are expanding our understanding of the ocean, its inhabitants, and its role in global climate systems.

In archaeology, AI is helping to uncover the secrets of our past. AI algorithms can analyze satellite imagery and geospatial data to identify potential archaeological sites, often revealing hidden structures or features undetectable to the human eye. This technology can assist archaeologists in planning field investigations while preserving cultural heritage.

Despite the significant advancements driven by AI in scientific discovery, it's crucial to approach its implementation thoughtfully. Researchers and institutions must remain aware of the risk of widening the gap between those with access to these powerful tools and those without. Balancing the immense potential of AI with these considerations will be key to fully realizing the benefits of AI in scientific discovery.

| 18 |

AI in Healthcare

AI has emerged as a game-changing technology in the healthcare industry, revolutionizing the way we diagnose, treat, and manage diseases. With its ability to process vast amounts of data, learn from patterns, and make predictions, it is improving patient outcomes, and enabling personalized medicine, creating new possibilities and challenges. From diagnostics to treatment planning, patient care, and research, AI holds the potential to significantly enhance healthcare delivery and outcomes.

I have no doubt that AI will enhance diagnosis, and treatment, and usher in a new era of personalized medicine. But, bringing about these medical miracles isn't a sprint, it's a marathon. It requires rigorous testing, complex healthcare data, stringent regulations, and a thorough ethical review. Think of it as building a skyscraper. It takes time, multiple checks and balances, and compliance with strict rules. Patient privacy and the ethical use of AI in healthcare will have to be considered.

Google's DeepMind, for instance, utilizes an AI system that interprets retinal images to detect early signs of diabetic retinopathy, a predominant cause of blindness. This results in more timely interventions and can help prevent vision loss.

AI algorithms have proven invaluable in the classification of medical images, such as X-rays, CT scans, and MRIs. They can discern benign from malignant lung nodules, identify specific fracture types, or distinguish between various cancer stages. In addition to classification, it also enhances the segmentation of medical images, highlighting specific structures or regions that require attention, such as tumors, organs, blood vessels, or other anatomical structures. This aids in delivering more accurate diagnoses and facilitates efficient treatment planning.

Predictive analytics, empowered by AI, analyzes extensive datasets of medical images and patient data to discern patterns and forecast outcomes. The AI algorithms can predict disease progression, treatment response, or risk of complications based on imaging findings and individual patient characteristics.

It also serves as a valuable second opinion for radiologists, offering additional insights and recommendations to enhance diagnostic accuracy and minimize errors. It streamlines radiology workflows by automating routine tasks such as image triage, prioritization, and report generation, freeing up radiologists to focus on more complex cases and reducing turnaround times.

The quality of medical images can be significantly improved with AI algorithms. Aidoc, an AI system, uses deep learning algorithms to scrutinize CT scans and pinpoint potential abnormalities. They are capable of noise reduction, contrast enhancement, and resolution improvement, enabling radiologists to better visualize subtle anomalies and enhance their overall image interpretation. Automated anomaly detection powered by AI can flag abnormalities in medical images. This assists radiologists in diagnosing diseases by drawing attention to tumors, lesions, fractures, or other peculiarities that may warrant further investigation. For example, they can automatically measure tumor size or volume, or quantify perfusion or diffusion parameters. Thus, AI in radiology and medical imaging has established itself as an indispensable tool, augmenting the capabilities of radiologists and improving patient care outcomes.

In the field of drug discovery and development, traditionally characterized by lengthy timelines and high costs, AI has become a powerful catalyst. Employing deep learning models, it can scrutinize enormous volumes of biological data, including genomics and proteomics, to pinpoint potential drug targets. For instance, BenevolentAI employs AI algorithms to sift through vast biomedical literature and databases, leading to the discovery of new drug candidates for diseases like amyotrophic lateral sclerosis (ALS).

One significant breakthrough powered by AI is the discovery of the novel antibacterial compound, Abaucin. Researchers leveraged AI algorithms and machine learning techniques to analyze extensive data on chemical compounds and their efficacy against bacteria, including details on the molecular structures of compounds, their chemical properties, and known antibacterial activities. The AI algorithms discerned patterns and correlations between the compounds' chemical attributes and their antibacterial effects, generating predictive models that could evaluate the potential antibacterial activity of new compounds, even those not yet synthesized or tested.

For Abaucin, the AI screening process identified its potential as a new and effective antibacterial compound based on its molecular structure and predicted antibacterial activity. This marked a significant milestone, as Abaucin demonstrated potent antibacterial effects against a wide array of bacteria, including drug-resistant strains.

AI's role in this screening process proves transformative for several reasons. Its screening dramatically accelerates drug discovery by swiftly analyzing large quantities of chemical data, enabling researchers to prioritize the most promising compounds for further testing, thereby saving significant time and resources. The algorithms can discover potential drug candidates that might have been overlooked using conventional screening methods, unveiling new opportunities for the development of innovative antibacterial drugs. AI screening can potentially reduce the financial burden associated with drug discovery by minimizing the number of compounds needing laboratory synthesis and testing, thus increasing cost-effectiveness. AI screening transcends the boundaries of traditional screening methods, which are heavily dependent on prior knowledge and assumptions.

In essence, AI screening holds the promise to revolutionize the discovery of new antibacterial compounds and expedite the development of effective treatments against bacterial infections. It equips researchers with the ability to make data-driven decisions, identify promising candidates, and streamline the drug discovery process. This, in turn, improves patient outcomes and tackles the escalating challenge of antibiotic resistance.

When it comes to healthcare accessibility, AI is playing an instrumental role in bolstering healthcare accessibility and improving patient outcomes through remote patient monitoring systems and telemedicine. AI-equipped wearable devices continuously track vital signs, identifying any irregularities and alerting healthcare providers instantly. Such vigilant monitoring paves the way for timely intervention and reduces the need for hospital readmissions.

One of the significant advantages of AI is its ability to detect health issues at an early stage. Through constant monitoring of critical parameters like heart rate, blood pressure, and respiratory rate via wearable devices, AI algorithms can scrutinize patterns and abnormalities, enabling early detection of potential health problems and allowing swift medical intervention.

Ensuring medication adherence is another area where AI has proven beneficial. AI algorithms can monitor and enhance medication adherence by examining data from smart pill dispensers or medication tracking apps, reminding patients to take their medication on time, and notifying healthcare providers about any missed doses.

AI can also offer other personalized health recommendations by analyzing an array of patient data, including vital signs, activity levels, sleep patterns, and dietary habits. Such information can be used to suggest tailored exercise routines, dietary changes, and lifestyle modifications specific to a patient's needs. For example, Buoy Health's AI chatbot conducts symptom assessments and provides users with suitable healthcare recommendations, minimizing unnecessary emergency room visits.

AI also assists in remote rehabilitation by guiding patients through exercises, providing real-time feedback on their movements, ensuring correct exercise performance, and tracking progress over time.

Virtual assistants powered by AI can serve as a valuable resource for patients, providing them with comprehensive information about their conditions and treatments. Besides answering queries, these virtual assistants can also schedule appointments, issue reminders, and offer general healthcare advice.

Diagnosing cancer at an early stage has always been crucial to a patient's survival. AI has improved diagnosing cancer through the analysis of medical images or patient data, revealing patterns and abnormalities far quicker and more accurately than humans can. IBM's Watson for Oncology stands as an example of this, demonstrating remarkable proficiency in providing personalized treatment plans. It analyzes patient data, sifts through vast amounts of medical literature, and follows treatment guidelines to aid oncologists, leading to improved outcomes.

When it comes to cancer detection, AI algorithms provide invaluable assistance by analyzing a variety of medical images such as mammograms, CT scans, and pathology slides. This helps in the early detection of diverse forms of cancer, including breast, lung, and skin cancers. IDx-DR, an AI-powered system, was developed specifically to detect diabetic retinopathy, utilizing the analysis of retinal images.

The integration of AI into precision oncology has marked a new era of personalized medicine, where treatments are tailored to individual patient characteristics. By analyzing genomic data, AI algorithms can pinpoint specific mutations and predict how a patient will respond to treatment. For instance, the Memorial Sloan Kettering Cancer Center's AI-powered clinical decision support system, MSK-IMPACT, assists oncologists in selecting targeted therapies aligned with each patient's unique genetic profile.

AI's application in treatment planning is proving highly beneficial, particularly in devising personalized treatment strategies. AI algorithms have the ability to consider a comprehensive range of data that includes a patient's medical history, genetic makeup, and lifestyle factors. By processing this diverse and expansive data set, AI can identify the most effective treatments for individual patients.

In doing so, AI manages to untangle the intricate combinations of variables that influence treatment effectiveness, a task that would be extraordinarily challenging, if not impossible, for humans. This ability to efficiently manage a vast amount of data and find personalized solutions significantly enhances the potential for positive treatment outcomes and patient well-being.

Besides improving diagnostics and care, AI has been instrumental in streamlining healthcare operations by automating administrative tasks, thereby reducing paperwork and enhancing efficiency. The use of Natural Language Processing (NLP) algorithms, for instance, allows for the extraction of information from medical records, leading to faster and more accurate coding and billing procedures. It has also been employed to optimize appointment booking systems, ensuring resources are allocated efficiently and waiting times are reduced. The integration of AI into healthcare operations not only expedites administrative tasks but also contributes to overall improved patient care by allowing healthcare providers to dedicate more time to direct patient interactions.

Once again, the use of AI in healthcare also raises important ethical issues. For instance, patient data privacy is a major concern. As AI systems require large amounts of data to function effectively, it is crucial to ensure this data is handled securely and confidentially. Additionally, there is the question of bias in AI decision-making. For instance, if the data used to train AI systems is biased, if it includes more data from one demographic group than another, the AI system may also display biased behavior. This can result in unfair or inaccurate medical outcomes.

While AI's role in healthcare is rapidly expanding, and while it holds immense potential, careful thought must be given to these ethical considerations. Only then can we ensure that the use of AI in healthcare is not only effective but also fair and respectful of patient rights.

| 19 |

AI in Mental Health

AI in the field of mental health is also opening up new avenues for assessment and treatment. It holds promise in enhancing the accuracy of diagnosis, broadening the reach of therapeutic interventions, and personalizing mental health care based on individual needs.

Research Acceleration with AI can expedite mental health research by analyzing datasets from various sources, such as electronic health records, clinical trial data, genomic data, and more. This can lead to new insights into the causes of mental health conditions, the effectiveness of treatments, and potential biomarkers for these conditions. For instance, AI can assist in identifying genetic variants associated with mental illnesses.

AI can also serve as a supportive tool for mental health professionals by assisting in tasks like diagnosis, treatment planning, and patient monitoring. For instance, AI algorithms can help psychiatrists and therapists analyze patient data to identify risk factors, predict treatment responses, and track progress over time. This can help professionals make more informed decisions and provide better care.

Preventative mental health care can also benefit from AI. By analyzing data on an individual's behavior, lifestyle, and environmental factors, AI can identify patterns suggestive of increased risk for mental health conditions. By spotting patterns and correlations in data, AI can aid in early detection and intervention, potentially preventing the escalation of these conditions.

This can allow for early interventions and preventive measures, reducing the likelihood of developing these conditions.

In the era of digitalization, AI-backed teletherapy platforms have emerged, which allow mental health professionals to provide services remotely. This can increase access to mental health services, particularly for individuals in remote areas or those who might be hesitant to seek in-person care due to stigma.

AI chatbots and virtual assistants are increasingly being used to deliver cognitive-behavioral therapy, a form of treatment that helps individuals change harmful thinking patterns. These AI-powered tools can offer support at any time, reducing the barriers to seeking help, and providing users with privacy and anonymity.

Facebook's proactive detection tool scans posts and comments for signs of suicidal thoughts based on pattern recognition. When potential patterns are detected, the system alerts a human moderator who can then provide tailored mental health resources to the user in question or their friends.

Woebot, which I mentioned earlier, is an AI-powered chatbot that employs principles of cognitive-behavioral therapy to detect early signs of anxiety and depression in users. The AI system learns from interactions with the user to provide timely interventions and suggest self-help tools.

Wysa, an AI-enabled mental health chatbot, applies cognitive-behavioral therapy techniques to assist users in managing conditions like anxiety, depression, and sleep disorders. The system uses machine learning algorithms to adjust its strategies based on the user's responses, helping them build effective coping mechanisms over time.

Quartet, a healthcare technology company, harnesses AI to bridge the gap between primary care doctors and mental health specialists. Its platform employs machine learning to identify patients potentially suffering from undiagnosed or untreated mental health conditions and recommends appropriate specialist care.

Ginger.io is an AI-backed app that identifies patterns in users' moods, sleep, and other behaviors to provide real-time, personalized mental health support. It connects users with human coaches when necessary, using the data analyzed by the AI system to guide the coaching process.

Ellipsis Health harnesses the power of AI to analyze users' speech and vocal patterns, using these as biomarkers for mental health. Their AI system assists healthcare providers in tracking patients' progress, enabling the adjustment of treatment plans based on the patient's current state.

Despite these potential benefits, again, ensuring data privacy and security is paramount since the confidentiality of mental health data is highly sensitive. Robust policies and regulations should be in place to protect the privacy and confidentiality of mental health data.

While AI can be a useful tool in mental health care, it can't replace the human touch entirely. The empathy, understanding, and therapeutic alliance that develop in a human-to-human therapeutic relationship are difficult, if not impossible, to replicate with AI. It is important to ensure that AI serves as a supplement to, not a replacement for, human mental health professionals, preserving the essential human connection and empathy in mental health care.

As we continue to integrate AI into mental health care, it becomes crucial to navigate these issues carefully. The potential benefits of AI are immense, but they must be balanced with respect for privacy, fairness, and the irreplaceable value of human connection.

| 20 |

AI and Accessibility

AI is a powerful tool that's making our world more inclusive. By providing innovative solutions for people with disabilities, it is not only enhancing accessibility but also empowering individuals to lead more independent and fulfilling lives. As it continues to evolve, we can look forward to even more breakthroughs in this field, making our society more accessible and inclusive for everyone. By incorporating AI, we can design solutions that empower individuals, accommodating their unique needs and experiences.

The potential that AI technology offers to assist those with disabilities is incredible. For example, it can convert speech to text and vice versa, facilitating communication for the hearing or speech impaired. Vision enhancement tools empowered by AI can help those with visual impairments navigate their surroundings and provide new means to perceive and interact with the world. Predictive text and gesture recognition can provide more effective communication tools for individuals with motor impairments. The capabilities in this regard are extensive and continually evolving.

AI is also innovating accessibility for individuals with hearing impairments, making auditory information more accessible.

Microsoft's Seeing AI, an application leveraging computer vision technology, acts as a verbalizing camera, describing objects, people, and text to visually impaired users, enhancing their interaction with their surroundings. OrCam MyEye is another AI-powered wearable device, that converts visual data into audible information in real time. This gives visually impaired users the ability to comprehend written text, recognize familiar faces, and identify everyday objects.

For the hearing impaired, Google's Live Transcribe instantly transcribes spoken words into text, allowing people with hearing impairments to actively participate in conversations, meetings, or lectures. Ava by Apple uses your smartphone's mic to transcribe voice-to-text, facilitating communication for deaf and hard-of-hearing individuals by providing real-time transcription of conversations.

For people that struggle with mobility impairments, AI is pushing the boundaries, enabling them to navigate spaces that were previously challenging. Google's Lookout employs AI to detect potential obstacles and provide vocal alerts, supporting individuals with mobility impairments in safely traversing their environment.

Exoskeletons equipped with AI are even helping individuals regain mobility. The embedded AI interprets the user's movement intentions, aiding in smooth, natural movement. Robotic exoskeletons are paving the way for enhanced mobility and independence, particularly amongst the aging population. Essentially functioning as wearable suits, these devices have the potential to provide strength where the body may not, facilitating the performance of tasks that could otherwise be challenging due to age-related physical constraints.

There are also applications for increasing strength and ability for physically demanding tasks. Augsburg-based startup German Bionic is one of several companies pioneering the development of wearable exoskeletons that provide superhuman strength and support. These cutting-edge devices, fueled by electric motors and equipped with AI technology, are capable of detecting a user's motions and administering supplementary strength precisely when and where it's needed, such as in the back, core, and legs. This harmony of machine and human effort helps enhance performance and safeguard against potential injuries.

AI is also providing valuable support to individuals with cognitive impairments, fostering greater independence. Google's Action Blocks use AI to simplify smartphone interactions. Users can craft personalized buttons for routine actions, like contacting a relative or managing smart home devices. Empowered Brain, an AI-enabled system by Brain Power, assists children with autism in honing their social and cognitive skills. Using Google Glass, the system provides social cues, helping them understand and react appropriately in social settings.

For those with speech impairments, AI is contributing to more accessible communication.

Google's Project Euphonia employs AI to comprehend and interpret unconventional speech patterns, granting people with speech impairments the freedom to communicate more expressively. Voiceitt, a speech recognition application, is tailored to understand non-standard speech patterns, enabling individuals with speech impairments to communicate using their unique voices.

As I will repeat throughout this book, there is always a critical ethical dimension to consider. While AI can help bridge accessibility gaps, it is also important to ensure that AI systems themselves are accessible and inclusive. It's not sufficient enough to create AI tools for individuals with disabilities. Instead, these individuals should be included in the development process, ensuring the AI tools are genuinely fit for purpose and respectful of the user's autonomy and privacy.

Accessibility should not be an afterthought in AI development but a key design principle. This would involve a shift towards universal design, creating products usable by all people without the need for adaptation. This approach ensures that AI tools are not just beneficial for people with disabilities but enhance usability for everyone. While AI holds considerable promise for improving accessibility and inclusion in the digital world, we have to navigate the ethical landscape, respecting rights and ensuring inclusivity in design and implementation.

| 21 |

AI in Warfare and Autonomous Weapons

AI has undeniably become a strategic asset in modern warfare. From autonomous weaponry to surveillance, intelligence, and reconnaissance, AI is revolutionizing military operations. These AI-powered systems can operate without human intervention, making critical decisions like identifying and engaging targets.

One aspect of this transformation is the speed and efficiency brought by AI in warfare. The use of automated drones and missile systems could potentially reduce risks to human soldiers and increase the precision of attacks, thus minimizing collateral damage. AI can analyze data quickly, enabling quicker responses to threats and improving strategic planning.

AI has proven its effectiveness through initiatives like the U.S. Department of Defense's Project Maven, which utilizes AI for drone footage analysis. Leveraging machine learning algorithms, the project can identify and categorize objects in the footage, reducing human analyst workloads and accelerating intelligence gathering. Additionally, it supports predictive analysis, aiding strategists in forecasting enemy movements and facilitating informed decision-making.

The emergence of autonomous weapon systems, capable of engaging targets without human intervention, is a contentious issue in the context of AI in warfare. Examples include the Israeli Harpy drone, which autonomously detects, attacks, and destroys radar emitters, and the U.S. Navy's Sea Hunter, an autonomous ship capable of tracking enemy submarines for prolonged periods without human assistance.

Cyber warfare is also being reshaped by AI. Machine learning algorithms are now capable of detecting network traffic anomalies, identifying potential threats, and responding at speeds unachievable by humans. For instance, the U.S. Defense Advanced Research Projects Agency (DARPA) has crafted an AI system, known as the Cyber Grand Challenge, that uses AI to identify and rectify software vulnerabilities.

Despite these advances, autonomous weapon systems pose a 'responsibility gap' issue, wherein accountability for potential unlawful actions becomes ambiguous. There are concerns about these weapons being susceptible to hacking or malfunctioning, which could inadvertently lead to casualties. There is a growing debate surrounding the absence of human judgment in life-or-death decisions. Many are advocating for a ban on lethal autonomous weapons, similar to the pre-existing ban on blinding lasers. The United Nations has convened multiple discussions on the topic, but a consensus is yet to be reached.

Who is responsible if an autonomous weapon system mistakenly targets civilians? This question brings into play the principles of accountability and liability, challenging traditional norms of warfare. How do we address the absence of human judgment and emotion in autonomous weapons? The human touch provides a level of control and moral decision-making that may be absent in autonomous AI systems. While AI can calculate probabilities and risks, it lacks human qualities like empathy and the capacity to fully understand the complex context of a conflict situation.

This lack of 'humanity' in decision-making processes could also lead to an escalation in warfare. If countries rely on AI systems that can engage without putting human lives at immediate risk, it might lower the threshold for going to war.

The proliferation of autonomous weapons and AI in warfare also presents a potential arms race scenario. As nations strive to outdo each other in military AI capabilities, it could lead to destabilization and heighten the risk of conflict.

I have no doubt that the use of AI in warfare and autonomous weapons will remain a contentious topic for some time. While the efficiency and protection of human soldiers are strong arguments for their use, the ethical implications cannot be ignored. It is essential to develop regulations and frameworks that ensure AI's responsible and ethical use in this arena.

| 22 |

AI and the Environment

Climate change is one of the most urgent issues of our time. In response, scientists are employing AI to better understand this complex phenomenon and predict its future impacts. Artificial Intelligence is poised to transform our approach to environmental conservation and sustainability. AI technologies, such as machine learning and predictive modeling, provide powerful tools for understanding and addressing environmental challenges.

For instance, AI can analyze vast amounts of climate data to predict weather patterns and model climate change scenarios. It can identify patterns that humans might overlook, helping scientists and policymakers make informed decisions about climate change mitigation strategies.

AI is also instrumental in wildlife conservation. Machine learning algorithms can analyze images from drones or satellite feeds to monitor wildlife populations and their habitats. By identifying changes in these images over time, AI can help detect threats such as deforestation, poaching, or changes in land use. Consider the open-source software, Wildbook, which employs AI to identify, catalog, and track individual animals using photographs. This advanced tool aids researchers in accurately mapping species populations and migration patterns, thereby formulating more effective conservation methods.

Notably, DeepMind by Google has crafted a machine learning model proficient in forecasting wind energy production 36 hours ahead of time, which helps optimize wind energy usage, curtail fossil fuel dependence, and reduce greenhouse gas emissions. It has created an AI system that has successfully cut down energy consumption in cooling its data centers by 40%, marking a substantial advancement in the pursuit of sustainable technology.

Similarly, predictive models are being created for air pollution, like IBM's Green Horizon Project. These AI and machine learning tools equip governments and organizations with critical data to act effectively against deteriorating air quality.

Efficiency in waste management is another domain that AI is revolutionizing. Recology, a startup based in San Francisco, uses AI for more precise waste sorting, which helps to diminish the volume of waste directed to landfills. AMP Robotics employs AI to enhance waste sorting and recycling efficiency, a use that not only decreases landfill waste but also aids in the conservation of valuable resources by correctly identifying and separating recyclable materials.

The potential for saving lives with AI by predicting weather patterns cannot be overstated. AI can scrutinize historical and real-time data to forecast weather patterns, like IBM's Deep Thunder which utilizes machine learning, big data, and cloud computing for precise, localized weather forecasts. Google's AI-driven flood forecasting system collects data from thousands of sensors and satellites, providing early flood warnings that can significantly decrease the potential loss of life and property.

The AI system developed by the University of Oklahoma leverages satellite data to predict droughts months in advance, a tool that can aid farmers and policymakers in making proactive decisions to mitigate the impacts of water shortages.

Tools like BreezoMeter employ AI to provide real-time air quality data, which empowers cities to respond swiftly and efficiently to pollution hazards, improving the health and well-being of their citizens.

Perhaps the most important and the most controversial is the use of AI in cloud seeding, a weather modification technique intended to create rain. AI algorithms enable greater precision and accuracy in identifying ideal conditions for cloud seeding, providing more accurate targeting of cloud formations. These advances in AI, combined with automation, also offer increases in efficiency, time, and resource savings. It also facilitates the scalability of cloud seeding initiatives, allowing for simultaneous monitoring and manipulation of various cloud systems, thus broadening the potential for generating significant precipitation increases.

AI's application in cloud seeding has critical future implications. By increasing rainfall in drought-stricken areas, AI-powered cloud seeding can mitigate the impacts of climate change. By manipulating cloud properties, it can help manage extreme weather events, reduce the severity of storms and hurricanes, and by extension, minimize property damage. AI's role in cloud seeding could also contribute to water resource management, addressing issues of water scarcity, and promoting sustainable development.

The potential environmental impact of altering precipitation patterns and cloud behavior is significant, necessitating continuous evaluation and monitoring. Altering precipitation patterns could disrupt ecosystems and harm biodiversity, potentially causing long-term damage. Chemicals used in cloud seeding, such as silver iodide, could potentially accumulate in the environment over time, leading to adverse effects. The control and predictability of cloud seeding are still new, with the potential for unintended consequences like unanticipated flooding.

Legally and ethically, the right to modify weather and the responsibility for unintended consequences remains contentious. If cloud seeding in one area influences weather patterns in another, this could trigger conflicts and disputes. Despite its usage for several decades, there's an ongoing debate about its effectiveness, compounded by the challenges of measuring success in weather modification experiments.

Another concern lies in the financial aspect of cloud seeding. The substantial investment required has led to criticisms suggesting that these resources could be better used for alternative water management strategies like conservation, infrastructure improvements, or desalination. There are also public health concerns regarding the potential impacts of cloud seeding chemicals. Although the quantities of substances like silver iodide used are generally considered safe, the potential risks of prolonged exposure continue to be a topic of debate.

In practice, AI's incorporation into cloud seeding has demonstrated promising results. The United Arab Emirates' Rain Enhancement Program, operational since 2017, has achieved significant increases in rainfall through AI integration. In the United States, the National Center for Atmospheric Research is developing Project Skywater, an AI-powered cloud seeding initiative.

AI's potency in aiding environmental conservation is just the tip of the iceberg. So what does the road ahead in Environmental Conservation look like? AI's potential to predict natural disasters more accurately could save lives and prevent property damage. It could also be pivotal in designing more efficient renewable energy systems and sustainable agriculture practices.

However, AI's potential shouldn't overshadow the fact that it isn't a panacea. It's a tool that should supplement other efforts to protect our environment.

As you can see, AI has tremendous potential to revolutionize environmental conservation but to fully utilize its benefits, we need continued innovation, ethical regulations, and a more comprehensive approach to environmental conservation. As we move toward a more digital future, AI emerges as a crucial ally in our pursuit of sustainability.

However, the use of AI comes with its own environmental implications. Training complex AI models requires substantial computational power, which in turn consumes large amounts of energy. The carbon footprint of AI technologies, therefore, can be quite significant. This brings to light the need for more energy-efficient AI technologies and the adoption of sustainable practices in AI research and development.

In addition, AI's ability to collect and analyze vast amounts of data also poses challenges. For example, satellite imagery used for environmental monitoring can infringe on the privacy of individuals and communities. How can we ensure that the data used for environmental purposes is gathered and used ethically? By leveraging its potential responsibly, we can harness the power of AI to protect our planet while mitigating the ethical and environmental risks associated with its use.

| 23 |

AI in Agriculture

The field of agriculture is no exception to industries AI is transforming. AI in agriculture involves the integration of advanced algorithms and machine learning capabilities to boost agricultural efficiency, productivity, and sustainability. As the global population continues to grow, ensuring food security is a pressing concern. AI provides innovative solutions to meet these challenges.

Precision agriculture is a farming management concept that uses AI and IoT (Internet of Things) devices to optimize field-level management. For instance, The Climate Corporation's FieldView software uses AI to analyze field data, giving farmers precise information about planting, managing, and harvesting crops. This approach minimizes resource wastage and maximizes crop yields.

AI-based laser tools are transforming the landscape of weed control in agriculture. These have the capability to identify and obliterate hundreds of thousands of weeds per hour with a precision that goes down to the sub-millimeter level. The system operates fully autonomously and can cover an impressive 15 to 20 acres per day, running around the clock.

The integration of AI in this manner facilitates sustainable farming practices, as it allows for enhanced crop growth without over-burdening our planet. It also substantially reduces labor costs and minimizes the use of chemicals by up to 95%. This is a significant step forward in reducing the environmental impact of agriculture.

AI is also used to monitor crop and soil health. Companies like Taranis use AI and deep learning tools to analyze high-resolution images of fields, providing farmers with early detection of crop diseases and pests. Similarly, Trace Genomics offers a soil analysis platform that uses machine learning to provide detailed soil health profiles, helping farmers understand their soil's potential and risks.

Farm equipment, such as tractors and drones, can now operate autonomously using AI technology. Companies like John Deere and Blue River Technology have developed "see and spray" machines that use computer vision to identify and spray weeds, reducing herbicide use by up to 80%. On the other hand, drones equipped with AI technology can perform tasks like planting seeds, fertilizing crops, and monitoring fields.

AI also aids in predictive analytics, allowing farmers to make more informed decisions. IBM's Watson Decision Platform for Agriculture merges AI with weather data and IoT devices to provide farmers with predictive insights. These insights help farmers understand weather patterns, crop stress, pest infestation risks, and soil conditions, allowing them to make data-driven decisions.

Just as a Fitbit collects data on a person's heart rate, steps, and sleep patterns, Cowlar collects key data about cows' behaviors and physiological parameters. This includes information about the cow's body temperature, activity levels, eating habits, and overall health status.

By tracking these metrics, the AI in Cowlar can detect anomalies that might indicate a potential health issue. For example, a sudden decrease in a cow's activity levels or changes in body temperature could signal that the animal is unwell. In such cases, Cowlar's system alerts the farmer, allowing for timely intervention and treatment. It can provide insights into the reproductive cycle of cattle, helping farmers optimize breeding practices. It can detect heat cycles with high accuracy, thus improving the success rate of breeding efforts and reducing the cost and stress associated with missed cycles.

Overall, the application of AI in livestock farming is about more than just monitoring and alerting. It's about equipping farmers with the insights they need to enhance livestock well-being, increase productivity, and make their operations more efficient and sustainable. It goes beyond enhancements in efficiency, resource conservation, and yield amplification. It leverages precise data and predictive analytics to minimize wastage and optimize productivity, thereby contributing to a sustainable and secure food production system. This helps counteract the effects of climate change on agriculture. It can also lessen the heavy labor demands associated with farming, making the industry more appealing to younger generations and addressing labor scarcities.

As the global population continues to rise, the demand for food will only increase. AI provides a promising solution to meet this demand sustainably and efficiently. By integrating AI into agriculture, we can create a more resilient, productive, and sustainable food system. The fusion of technology and agriculture holds immense potential, and with the right policies and investments, we can harness this potential for a better future. Nonetheless, potential challenges need to be taken into account, such as the requirement for digital infrastructure, farmer education, and the need to handle ethical and privacy issues.

| 24 |

AI in the Financial Sector

The financial sector is a hotbed for AI due to the vast amounts of data generated daily. From credit card transactions to stock market movements, every action creates a data point that can be analyzed and used to predict future trends. AI algorithms can process this data at record speeds, making real-time financial decision-making a reality. By leveraging AI technologies, these institutions can now make better predictions, automate processes, and provide personalized services to their customers.

AI's speed in detecting fraudulent activities is remarkable, significantly reducing the time between the fraud occurrence and its detection. This prompt action prevents further fraudulent transactions, safeguarding customers' accounts. AI has improved detection accuracy, leading to a significant reduction in false positives. This has enhanced the overall customer experience, as customers don't have to deal with unnecessary alerts for legitimate transactions.

Despite the significant strides made by AI in fraud detection, there are some challenges and limitations to consider. First and foremost, AI systems rely heavily on data for accurate predictions. Any inaccuracies or inconsistencies in the data can lead to false negatives or positives, impacting the effectiveness of the system. Additionally, implementing and maintaining AI systems can be costly. This could pose a significant barrier for small and medium-sized enterprises that may not have the financial resources to invest in such advanced technology. While AI has revolutionized fraud detection, it's important to address these challenges for it to become a universally accessible solution.

Machine learning and artificial intelligence are powerful tools for detecting stock market fraud. The SEC's MIDAS is a great example of this, as it uses high-frequency trading data to look for abnormal patterns that might indicate fraudulent activity. By analyzing millions of transactions per second, the system can identify unusual trading behavior that may be indicative of market manipulation, insider trading, or other illegal activities. This impressive system showcases how AI can enhance regulatory enforcement and protect investors by ensuring fairness and transparency in the financial markets. AI has the potential to revolutionize the way financial fraud is detected and prevented, but it also requires careful oversight and regulation to ensure its proper and ethical use.

In the investment banking sector, it's employed in algorithmic trading for high-speed and high-volume transactions that surpass human capacity. It also serves a vital role in predictive forecasting by scrutinizing market trends and projecting future fluctuations. Risk assessment is another arena where AI steps in to recognize and gauge potential risk factors.

Despite its many uses, the construction of precise and dependable AI models can prove to be complex and expensive. There's the hazard of becoming overly dependent on AI, which can result in substantial losses if the AI's prognostications are off the mark. AI's involvement in high-frequency trading has received backlash for stoking market volatility. The potential for bias in AI algorithms is a growing concern, as it may lead to unjust or unethical results.

AI can also analyze customer behavior and spending patterns to provide personalized banking products and services. For instance, based on a customer's spending habits, AI can suggest the most suitable credit card or loan product. It can also help banks identify up-selling or cross-selling opportunities, thereby enhancing customer satisfaction and boosting profitability.

Legal concerns have also emerged in the financial sector concerning the use of AI. A case in point is the 2018 incident involving Equifax and TransUnion, two of the largest credit reporting agencies in the U.S. The Consumer Financial Protection Bureau levied fines against these entities for allegedly misleading consumers in the marketing of credit scores and products. These agencies were utilizing AI and machine learning for credit risk prediction but were accused of lacking transparency in their models and potentially practicing discrimination.

Such disputes underscore the imperative for transparency, accountability, and ethical considerations in the application of AI. It's crucial that AI algorithms are developed and deployed responsibly to prevent unfair outcomes and maintain public trust. AI systems used for credit scoring or loan approval might make decisions based on biased data, leading to discrimination against certain demographic groups. If an AI system makes a wrong prediction or decision, it can have serious financial consequences for individuals and businesses. However, due to the complexity of these systems, it can be challenging to understand how they arrived at a particular decision.

| 25 |

AI in Social Media

In the digital age, social media platforms have become an integral part of our daily lives, shaping how we connect, communicate, and consume information. With the rapid advancement of AI, social media has evolved beyond a mere communication tool, transforming into a powerful platform that leverages AI capabilities to enhance user experiences, deliver personalized content, and even combat harmful content. However, as with any AI technology, there are both benefits and pitfalls associated with the integration of AI in social media.

AI's influence on social media is profound, offering benefits such as enhanced personalization, efficient content moderation, and advanced sentiment analysis. These algorithms can dissect vast amounts of user data to ascertain preferences, interests, and behavior patterns. This analysis allows platforms to curate personalized content, streamline advertisements, and provide more meaningful recommendations, thereby refining user experiences. For instance, Facebook employs AI to generate personalized news feeds, displaying posts in line with users' interests and engagement habits.

It also aids in moderating and filtering content on social media platforms, a task that can prove overwhelming due to the immense volume of user-generated content. AI-driven tools can efficiently scrutinize and flag potentially harmful or inappropriate content, easing the burden on human moderators. For example, YouTube utilizes AI to detect and expunge videos that breach its community guidelines, creating a safer environment for users.

AI sentiment analysis offers platforms an understanding of users' emotions, opinions, and feedback. Such insights allow businesses and brands to gauge customer sentiment and adjust their marketing tactics accordingly. Twitter, for example, leverages sentiment analysis algorithms to monitor public opinion and trend progression, enabling businesses to gauge real-time public reactions to products, services, or events.

Despite these advantages, integrating AI into social media brings certain challenges such as privacy concerns, algorithmic bias, and the propagation of misinformation and fake news. The handling of user data by AI raises serious privacy issues as this information is collected, analyzed, and applied in decision-making processes. The management and storage of this data must adhere to stringent privacy regulations and uphold transparency to safeguard users' personal information. Facebook's controversy surrounding its treatment of user data underscores the necessity for enhanced privacy protocols in AI-integrated social media platforms.

Since AI algorithms learn from historical data, they may internalize inherent biases, which, if unchecked, could perpetuate discrimination, reinforce stereotypes, and constrain diversity on social media platforms. Twitter's image cropping algorithm's bias towards lighter-skinned individuals exemplifies the need to address these biases to ensure fair and inclusive platform experiences.

In addition, AI algorithms risk amplifying misinformation and fake news by promoting sensational or contentious content. This presents a substantial challenge in upholding the integrity of shared information on social media platforms. The criticisms faced by social media platforms for the spread of misinformation during the 2016 U.S. presidential election, and the role AI algorithms played in escalating false information, underscore this concern.

The issue of AI-generated fake news and misinformation has become a significant concern. AI can create convincingly real deep-fake videos, or generate misleading news articles, which can spread rapidly on social media platforms. This can have serious implications, including political manipulation and social discord.

There are also concerns about AI's role in encouraging echo chambers. As AI tends to suggest content based on a user's existing views and preferences, users may end up in a feedback loop, seeing only content they agree with and isolating them from differing perspectives.

Legal controversies involving AI and social media have surfaced over the years. A significant instance I mentioned earlier is the Cambridge Analytica scandal where Facebook was implicated in employing AI algorithms to harvest and analyze personal data from millions of users without their explicit consent. This significant privacy violation led to several lawsuits against Cambridge Analytica and Facebook alike.

Another notable case involves Tay, an AI chatbot crafted by Microsoft for interaction with Twitter users. The bot was programmed to learn from ongoing conversations. However, it started generating offensive tweets within a few hours of its launch after engaging with malicious users. This situation underscored the pressing ethical issues associated with AI use on social media platforms.

Social media platforms have been embroiled in legal disputes concerning algorithmic bias. Content curation and personalization algorithms have been accused of endorsing discriminatory or damaging content. For instance, YouTube faced a lawsuit in 2019 over allegations of promoting extremist content via its recommendation algorithm.

Lawsuits have also arisen from the dissemination of AI-manipulated deepfake videos on social media. deepfakes employ AI technology to superimpose one individual's face onto another's body in a video, falsely portraying the former's actions or words. These doctored videos have been weaponized for harmful intents, including spreading false information and defaming individuals. Such legal actions underscore the necessity for comprehensive regulations and guidelines to ensure responsible and ethical AI applications within social media platforms.

AI has undoubtedly revolutionized social media, offering numerous benefits such as enhanced personalization, efficient content moderation, and advanced sentiment analysis. However, challenges including privacy concerns, algorithmic bias, and the spread of misinformation must be addressed to ensure the responsible and ethical use of AI in social media. By leveraging the potential of AI while remaining vigilant and accountable, we can create a social media landscape that is more inclusive, trustworthy, and beneficial for users worldwide.

| 26 |

AI in the Legal and Justice System

It should come as no surprise that AI has been elbowing its way into the justice system, finding applications in a variety of areas including sentencing guidance, crime prediction, case management, and legal research. It's become an integral part of the legal process, attempting to aid in estimating recidivism rates, assisting in evidence discovery, and streamlining legal research.

One notable area where AI is utilized is in risk assessment algorithms. These algorithms are designed to predict the likelihood of a defendant engaging in future criminal activity. Judges often rely on these predictions to make crucial decisions about bail, sentencing, and parole. However, this has raised some concerns. There is ongoing debate about the accuracy and fairness of these algorithms. There's a growing concern that these algorithms could perpetuate racial and socioeconomic biases embedded in the data they're trained on, which poses significant ethical challenges.

Predictive policing, a practice that involves using algorithms to anticipate crime, might sound like something straight out of a sci-fi movie. But it's real, and it's being used right now in different cities across the globe. While it seems cutting-edge and innovative, there are some pretty significant concerns to consider here.

There is one huge glaring problem of data bias. These algorithms rely on historical crime data to make their predictions. But this data is often skewed. Why? Because if law enforcement has been patrolling certain neighborhoods more than others in the past, more crime is likely to be reported in these areas. This doesn't necessarily mean there's actually more crime happening there, just that more crime gets detected.

So, when this skewed data is fed into the predictive policing algorithms, it means cops keep being sent back to the same neighborhoods. This becomes a cycle or a feedback loop. More cops lead to more arrests, which then gets marked as more crime data, sending even more cops to the same place. This creates a self-fulfilling prophecy.

This often ends up affecting marginalized communities the most. If a neighborhood is predominantly home to people of color, immigrants, or the unhoused, and it's been heavily policed in the past, predictive policing can potentially lead to an increase in the over-policing of these communities.

Real-life examples of this are not hard to find. In Los Angeles, the use of PredPol resulted in an increase in police activity in minority neighborhoods. In Chicago, a predictive algorithm was used to flag individuals who had been victims of a crime or knew people who had committed crimes. This means that people were being placed on the police's radar based on where they lived or who they knew, not on anything they had done.

Let me give you a frightening, but very real example. On December 12, 2017, a 23-year-old man was shot and killed in Chicago. In the wake of this incident, the Chicago Police Department (CPD) initiated an investigation, which extended into social media, not only about the victim but also those publicly grieving his sudden death. The CPD's data collection included social media content of individuals expressing their grief.

This data collection strategy was disclosed by a range of internal documents, which the ACLU of Illinois and Lucy Parsons Labs, a Chicago-based non-profit focused on police transparency and accountability, had obtained via FOIA requests. These documents reveal CPD's strategy of monitoring the social media accounts of victims of gun violence, as well as those of their friends and family members. While the stated aim of this surveillance is to garner more information about shootings, it has been found that CPD also accumulates public social media content from individuals who seemingly have little to no direct connection with the crime in question. The collection of documents covers non-consecutive 12 months ranging from November 2017 to July 2019.

Judges have been using the AI-driven software COMPAS to determine recidivism (the likelihood an individual will break the law again) which can seriously impact sentencing decisions. In 2016, Julia Angwin, a technology reporter, and her team at ProPublica did a deep dive into more than 7,000 COMPAS assessments from Broward County, Florida. Their investigation started sounding some alarms, suggesting that COMPAS was tipping the scales against African Americans. Their research found that African Americans were almost twice as likely as whites to be slapped with a high-risk label but then not actually re-offend. On the flip side, COMPAS was more likely to do the complete opposite with whites, branding them as lower-risk, only for them to go on and commit more crimes. They found it to be less accurate than random human assessment.

In the spring of 2014, 18-year-old Brisha Borden found herself late for a school pick-up when she noticed an unlocked blue Huffy bicycle and a silver Razor scooter. Borden, along with a companion, decided to borrow the small-sized conveyances, only to be confronted by the rightful owner, a mother claiming them as her child's property. Despite immediately abandoning the items, a neighbor alerted law enforcement, and both girls were arrested for burglary and petty theft.

In a comparable case from the previous summer, 41-year-old Vernon Prater was apprehended for stealing tools worth $86.35 from a local Home Depot. Prater, a repeat offender with a history of armed robbery, was a stark contrast to Borden, whose criminal record was limited to juvenile misdemeanors. Yet, when both were processed at the jail, a computer program designed to predict future criminal activities surprisingly rated Borden, a black female, as a high risk and Prater, a white male, as a low risk.

Fast forward two years and the algorithm's predictions were proven incorrect. Borden had not faced any new charges, while Prater had received an eight-year sentence for a warehouse break-in.

This brings to light concerns that predictive policing could further embed biases already present in the criminal justice system. These prediction models rely heavily on historical crime data, and any bias within this data, such as over-policing in specific neighborhoods or racial profiling, might get reflected and possibly amplified in the predictions. Such models can then create a cycle of self-fulfilling prophecy, with more arrests reinforcing the algorithm's predictions.

For instance, Chicago's Strategic Subject List, a program aimed at predicting individuals likely to be involved in shootings, has elicited privacy concerns. Surveillance tools like Dataminr, Geofeedia, and TransVoyant, funded by In-Q-Tel, the CIA's venture capital arm. It is used for monitoring social media posts and raises significant privacy concerns. As awareness grows about these issues, actions are being taken, as evidenced by Santa Cruz, California's decision in June 2020 to become the first U.S. city to ban predictive policing.

So, as cool as it may sound to have a crystal ball predicting crime, we have to consider the serious implications it could have on over-policing and racial profiling. As with all powerful tools, it's important to consider not just how it can be used, but how it might be misused. When we rely too much on these tools, we run the risk of reinforcing biases, alienating communities, and creating an Orwellian society where everyone's a suspect. That's a future we can do without.

The rise of AI in the legal sector, particularly in case management, introduces significant opportunities and accompanying complexities. The ability of AI to efficiently sift through large volumes of documents, extract critical details, and systematically organize them has transformed numerous aspects of the legal process. AI applications are able to predict case outcomes and provide invaluable insights to inform strategic decisions. Balancing the transformative potential of AI with these challenges means we need robust scrutiny, regulation, and an ongoing commitment to uphold fairness and justice in its implementation.

Platforms like ROSS Intelligence and LexisNexis use AI to analyze vast quantities of legal documents and provide comprehensive, up-to-date information to support lawyers in their research. However, while AI can scan and comprehend thousands of legal documents, it might miss critical cases or legal subtleties that a trained lawyer would recognize. Additionally, the reliance on existing case law could potentially inhibit innovative legal arguments.

AI-powered chatbots like DoNotPay have facilitated access to legal services for individuals who can't afford a lawyer by successfully challenging parking tickets and similar minor infractions. However, these AI tools cannot entirely replace the expertise and advice of a human lawyer, particularly for complex legal matters.

Tools like TurboPatent use AI to automate and streamline the patent filing process, which can significantly reduce the time and costs involved. Nevertheless, there is a risk that these AI-based tools could overlook subtle nuances or complexities in patent laws, potentially leading to erroneous filings.

AI is also employed in dispute resolution, with platforms like Resolver using AI to mediate complaints between consumers and businesses. While the aim is to settle disputes before they escalate to legal action, there's the risk that AI may fail to comprehend the emotional nuances involved in disputes, potentially leading to unsatisfactory resolutions.

Platforms like LegalRobot simplify contract analysis using AI. However, while this platform can help with the heavy lifting of contract analysis, it might not grasp the subtleties of complex legal language or understand the intent of the parties, leading to potential misinterpretations.

The challenges often revolve around the ethical application of AI, its potential for bias, transparency of algorithms, and its impact on fundamental rights such as due process. In the case of State v. Loomis, several defendants in Wisconsin initiated legal proceedings against the state, contending that their rights to due process were violated due to the deployment of COMPAS during sentencing as it hinges on proprietary algorithms. Despite this, the Wisconsin Supreme Court upheld the usage of COMPAS, provided its limitations are clearly comprehended by the court.

Despite the glaring issues, there is potential for AI to improve the efficiency and fairness of the justice system. For instance, AI could help reduce human error and bias in legal decisions, improve access to legal services, and provide more accurate crime predictions for better resource allocation.

However, for AI to be a force for good in the justice system, stringent regulations and transparency are crucial. Policymakers and stakeholders need to engage in ongoing discussions about the ethical implementation of AI in the justice system. Without vigilant oversight, the use of AI could risk exacerbating existing biases and inequalities, rather than resolving them.

| 27 |

AI in Space Exploration

The field of space exploration is a testament to human ingenuity, and the introduction of artificial intelligence is pushing this domain to new frontiers. AI is not just a tool but a partner in our quest to understand the cosmos, aiding in tasks ranging from data analysis to piloting spacecraft.

Space travel and exploration present complex and hazardous operations that are well-suited for the application of AI. Consequently, professionals involved in these activities, from astronauts to scientists, increasingly depend on machine learning to manage both routine and extraordinary issues.

During spacecraft launch and landing, AI helps automate engine functions, including deploying landing gear, to optimize fuel consumption. SpaceX, for instance, employs an AI-driven autopilot system in its Falcon 9 rockets. This system autonomously performs intricate operations like docking with the International Space Station (ISS). By calculating the spacecraft's trajectory while considering factors like fuel usage, atmospheric interference, and the sloshing of engine fluids, the AI helps ensure efficient and accurate operations. These applications of AI exemplify its transformative impact on space travel, demonstrating its potential for enhancing efficiency, safety, and discovery.

Launched in December 2021, the James Webb Space Telescope (JWST) is a pioneering collaboration between NASA, the European Space Agency (ESA), and the Canadian Space Agency (CSA). In its brief operation, the JWST has already made significant discoveries, such as detecting the first clear evidence of carbon dioxide in an exoplanet's atmosphere and revealing what might be six ancient galaxies, termed "universe breakers", due to their potential to disrupt current cosmological theories. These revelations provide a window into the early Universe, just a few hundred million years post-Big Bang.

AI plays a crucial role in managing and analyzing the vast amounts of data generated by the JWST. AI's speed and precision in handling large datasets enable the rapid identification of patterns or anomalies, accelerating our understanding of the cosmos. It assists in the classification of celestial bodies, optimizing the telescope's operations, and even troubleshooting operational anomalies.

As AI continues to advance, its potential applications in predicting cosmic phenomena could provide a leap forward in space exploration, cementing its central role in realizing the full potential of the James Webb Space Telescope. The potential of AI to uncover knowledge about our universe that might have otherwise remained undiscovered due to human limitations is a game changer.

Communication in deep space has also seen advancements due to AI. NASA's Deep Space Network employs AI to predict and mitigate signal disruptions, maintaining seamless communication with distant spacecraft.

AI's capacity for real-time analysis and decision-making can prove critical in many situations in space exploration, such as when immediate adjustments are required to a spacecraft's course to avoid collision with space debris. Yes, this may sound like it is right out of an episode of Star Trek, but this rapid decision-making capacity can greatly enhance the safety and success rates of space missions. AI has also made critical contributions to spacecraft navigation and trajectory optimization. The ESA's Gaia mission leverages AI to plot efficient paths through space, reducing fuel usage and mission duration. Most importantly, it aids in autonomous collision detection and avoidance, ensuring the protection of valuable space assets.

AI-powered rovers and probes, such as NASA's Curiosity rover and the European Space Agency's (ESA) Philae probe, have revolutionized the study of celestial bodies. AI algorithms enable these devices to analyze images autonomously, select targets for further investigation, and navigate challenging terrains and operational scenarios. This is particularly important for missions far from Earth where communication delays make direct control impractical. For instance, the Mars rovers are equipped with AI systems that allow them to navigate the Martian terrain independently, analyzing the surroundings and deciding the best path to follow.

As we aim to send humans farther into space, AI will play a crucial role in maintaining spacecraft and ensuring astronaut safety. As these systems become more integral to human spaceflight, their reliability and transparency become even more important.

In the long term, the acceleration of scientific discoveries through AI will drive the advancement of our understanding of the universe. These advancements could have far-reaching implications, ranging from deepening our insights into the universe's origin and evolution to potentially discovering extraterrestrial life. In essence, the role of AI in processing and analyzing space data is a substantial leap forward in our capability to explore and comprehend the universe. The importance lies in its potential to profoundly enhance our knowledge and lead to breakthrough discoveries that could redefine our understanding of our place in the cosmos.

Since we are already pushing the boundaries of science fiction, let's take a peek at where AI could take us in the future of space exploration. Some of the exciting possibilities we envision include the development of advanced autonomous systems. With more sophisticated AI technology, we could engineer spacecraft fully capable of executing complex exploration missions, with no requirement for human intervention. These autonomous spacecraft could manage their resources, adapt to environmental shifts, and even undergo self-repair if necessary.

The most fascinating prospect for me is the role AI could play in deep space habitation. AI technology could be deployed to manage the life-sustaining systems of future deep-space habitats. It could monitor astronaut health and well-being, oversee resources, and automate routine tasks. By handling these daily operations, AI would free up crew members to devote their time and energy to more pressing research and exploration activities. While I find this intriguing for the advancement of mankind, my feet will remain firmly planted on this Earth. To those of you that will brave this new frontier, I salute you...from the ground.

For astrobiology and the hunt for extraterrestrial life, the potential of AI is immense. We could develop AI algorithms designed specifically to assess planetary conditions and scour for signs of life beyond Earth. Through machine learning, these algorithms could detect patterns or anomalies in data that might hint at the presence of life.

Let's just say that we do encounter extraterrestrial beings. AI's ability to decipher potentially intricate alien languages through pattern and structure analysis in signals or messages could prove invaluable. This ability would foster our understanding of and communication with them and potentially prevent catastrophic misunderstandings, which could lead to our own destruction. If advanced to encompass ethical decision-making algorithms, AI could also help guide us in making critical decisions about our interactions with these beings. These decisions could range from issues of non-interference to risk assessments associated with contact.

AI systems would be invaluable in quickly analyzing essential information about extraterrestrial beings, their technologies, their intentions, and their home environments, significantly enhancing our understanding and decision-making capacity in these unprecedented circumstances.

| 28 |

AI in Quantum Physics

I cannot start explaining how AI works with Quantum Physics until I try to explain what it is. Why? Because even experts in this area say that no one really understands it. Why is it important? Even if quantum physics seems odd and hard to understand, it's essential because it provides us with the tools to innovate and create technologies that we now take for granted, and it will undoubtedly be the foundation of many more advancements in the future.

"If you are not completely confused by quantum mechanics, you do not understand it."

— John Wheeler

"Quantum mechanics makes absolutely no sense."

— Roger Penrose

"I do not like it, and I am sorry I ever had anything to do with it."

— Erwin Schrodinger

"If it is correct, it signifies the end of physics as a science."

— Albert Einstein

"I think I can safely say that nobody understands quantum mechanics."

— Richard Feynman

I know I am not alone here when I say that quantum physics has always been a little above my pay grade. I had to spend quite a bit of time desperately trying to comprehend these concepts from my partner, husband, and co-author who is absolutely obsessed with it. Let me be really clear, I would not be able to write this chapter without him. I am going to do my best to explain it in very simple terms for the majority of you out there like me.

Quantum physics is like the rulebook for a magical world, but it's really for the smallest particles in the universe, like atoms and electrons. The rules are very different from what we see in our everyday life. For instance, there's a rule called 'superposition'. It's like a coin spinning in the air, not being just heads or tails, but both at once. Perhaps the most quoted example of superposition is Schrodinger's cat, which was a thought experiment proposed by physicist Erwin Schrödinger in 1935.

Imagine you have a cat, and you place it in a sealed box with a radioactive atom, a Geiger counter (which measures radioactivity), and a vial of poison. If the atom decays, the Geiger counter detects it and breaks the vial, releasing the poison and killing the cat. If the atom does not decay, the poison isn't released and the cat remains fluffy and alive.

Here's where it gets confusing. According to quantum mechanics, the radioactive atom can be in a superposition of states both decayed and not decayed at the same time until we actually check, or observe it. Because the cat's life depends on the state of the atom, it too becomes entangled with the atom's state, making the cat both dead and alive until we open the box to look.

However, in our everyday experience, we know that a cat must be either alive or dead, not both at the same time. This contradiction between quantum mechanics and our everyday experience is what Schrodinger wanted to highlight with his cat experiment. It's a way to think about the oddities of quantum mechanics and how they might apply (or not apply) to larger objects or systems, like cats and boxes.

Another magical rule is 'entanglement.' Let's say you have two dice. Normally, when you roll them, they each fall randomly. But in the quantum world, these dice could be 'entangled.' That means if one die rolls a six, the other one also rolls a six, no matter how far apart they are. It's like having two twin dice that always roll the same number at the exact same time, even if one is in your house and the other is at your friend's house across town.

Then there's 'wave-particle duality.' This is as if you could be both a person and a cartoon character at the same time. In the quantum world, light behaves this way - sometimes it acts like a particle (like a tiny dot), and other times it acts like a wave, like ripples in a pond. Sometimes, it can even act like both at the same time, until someone decides to measure it. Then it is either a wave or a particle.

Quantum physics might sound super weird, but remember, it's all about the rulebook for the universe's tiniest things. Scientists even use these strange rules to create cool stuff like super-fast quantum computers. Just like in a magical world, once you know the rules, you can do some amazing things.

It's not just about blowing our minds with weird and wonderful ideas, though. It has practical uses that have changed our daily lives. For example, the principles of quantum physics are at the core of technologies like lasers, which are used in everything from supermarket scanners to surgical equipment. It's also the science behind the development of computers and smartphones by allowing us to manipulate and understand materials at the tiniest scales.

This is where AI, especially machine learning, comes into play when trying to understand and manipulate these complex quantum systems. Because quantum physics is mathematically intricate and quantum systems can exist in a massive number of possible states, AI proves useful in managing this complexity. It aids in recognizing patterns and making predictions, designing new quantum experiments, anticipating their outcomes, and interpreting the results.

AI can also control quantum devices, such as quantum computers, by optimizing their functions and correcting errors. This intersection between AI and quantum physics even gives rise to a new field called "Quantum Machine Learning." In this field, quantum computers are used to enhance machine learning algorithms, potentially solving problems too difficult for conventional computers. This marriage of AI and quantum physics holds great promise, and it could lead to significant advancements in both fields, revolutionizing our understanding of the universe and the realm of computing.

Using this advanced technology is like taming a wild horse. The goal is to guide it in the direction you want it to go, but you have to deal with all the unpredictable moves it might make along the way. In the field of quantum physics, these unpredictable moves are caused by small disturbances from the environment around us, like temperature changes. These disturbances are called dampening or noise. Researchers from the Okinawa Institute of Science and Technology (OIST) in Japan have found a way to counteract this by using AI to tame these wild particles. They are using AI to understand and predict their moves just like a trainer using different methods to calm a wild horse, the AI uses what are called 'control pulses,' varying intensities of light and voltage to keep these tiny particles on track.

This is a big deal because when these particles behave predictably, they can be used in technology in really exciting ways. For example, they could be used to create ultra-sensitive sensors that could measure anything from gravity to tiny shifts in position.

However, to make the most of these particles, the researchers have to find a way to make them behave, despite the environmental noise. It's like trying to keep the horse calm in a storm. The AI they're using is learning to do this, and it's showing a lot of promise. The researchers are hopeful that this method will open up a lot of new opportunities in the future.

The pharmaceutical industry also has high hopes for using AI and quantum mechanics. Imagine scientists finding a new molecule that could potentially be used to create a new medicine. The traditional method used to gain an understanding of the form, dimensions, and even activities of this molecule involved transforming the molecule into a crystal and employing X-rays to obtain a 3D image. This process was lengthy and complicated.

In recent times, scientists started using computer programs to predict what this 3D picture would look like, a method based on quantum physics. This process, called crystal structure prediction (CSP), is still complex and takes up a lot of computer power, sometimes up to four months. However, a recent partnership with a tech company called XtalPi has helped Pfizer, a well-known pharmaceutical company, sped up this process dramatically. XtalPi's technology, which uses artificial intelligence and cloud computing, can solve the complex equations involved in CSP in just a few days. Pfizer, with its wealth of experience in the field, was one of the early collaborators with XtalPi, helping to refine these new techniques.

With this new method, Pfizer can now investigate almost every new molecule they come across much faster than before. This exciting advancement is already changing how Pfizer conducts its research and has the potential to significantly impact the whole pharmaceutical industry.

Just like the advent of self-driving cars was a huge leap forward in transportation technology, this method could be a massive step toward building self-controlling quantum machines. We're still in the early stages, but the future looks promising.

| 29 |

AI in Art and Creativity

One of the most commonly known uses of AI is for creative arts like image generation, music creation, and writing. AI systems can generate remarkable artworks, music compositions, and even literary pieces that challenge our understanding of creativity. There has been a lot of negative chatter about this online and in the news. Creative artists worry that AI will mimic their work, replace them, or make their industry more competitive.

One prominent manifestation of AI in art is through Generative Adversarial Networks (GANs). These AI systems can produce intricate and unique pieces of visual art. DeepDream, a brainchild of Google, represents one of the pioneering applications of AI in the realm of art. This tool leverages neural networks to morph ordinary images into surreal, dream-like visuals by enhancing specific patterns within the input.

Prisma is an AI-infused app that works magic on ordinary photographs, morphing them into exquisite art pieces reminiscent of renowned artists and various art styles. Prisma's underlying deep neural networks imbue user-submitted photos with different artistic styles, encouraging users to explore diverse artistic filters.

RunwayML is an innovative platform that assimilates various AI models into artistic processes. It enables artists to play with cutting-edge AI algorithms, creating dynamic visuals, interactive experiences, and acoustic compositions. By bridging the gap between AI and artistic expression, RunwayML unfolds new avenues of creativity for artists.

Midjourney, an AI-driven platform, specializes in video creation and editing. Utilizing its sophisticated algorithms and machine learning capacities, Midjourney enables the creation of high-quality videos with a user-friendly interface.

A highlight of Midjourney is its simplistic drag-and-drop mechanism, which simplifies video arrangement and editing. Users can conveniently incorporate transitions, effects, and textual overlays, culminating in a well-refined video.

The platform also automates aspects of video editing, such as color grading and audio adjustments, utilizing AI, thus saving users valuable time and effort. Advanced features like facial recognition and object tracking are integrated into Midjourney, fostering the creation of dynamic, interactive videos.

Drag Your GAN harnesses the power of Generative Adversarial Networks (GANs) to generate customizable digital art. Users can modify the AI-produced artwork in real time, offering a personalized artistic experience. For instance, you could take an image of yourself and change a from to smile, move your hands, or close your eyes.

The appeal of Drag Your GAN lies in its potential to mingle AI-generated art with human creativity, fostering a platform for users to experiment with different artistic styles. Its application extends beyond personal use to industries like graphic design, advertising, and entertainment, offering professionals a novel tool to create custom visuals aligning with their artistic vision.

Drag Your GAN demonstrates the promising fusion of AI and art by marrying the robustness of GANs with user interactivity. It empowers artists, designers, and creative professionals to push boundaries, explore their creativity, and generate stunning, personalized digital artwork.

In the field of music, AI is used to compose pieces across various genres, often indistinguishable from those created by humans. AI can analyze musical patterns, styles, and structures from extensive databases of songs to generate new compositions, even mimicking the styles of famous composers or artists.

An AI composer called Aiva crafts original pieces of classical music. By dissecting a comprehensive library of musical compositions, Aiva's deep learning algorithms generate harmonious tunes, aiding composers in their creative process and even collaborating with human musicians to fabricate striking pieces.

Artisto, akin to Prisma but dedicated to videos, employs artistic filters to concoct visually compelling animated clips. Artisto's AI algorithms metamorphose ordinary videos into animated, artistic marvels, instilling artistic flair into everyday moments.

Artificial intelligence has also made its way into the world of literature, transforming the creative process and enhancing storytelling. OpenAI's GPT is a highly advanced language model leveraging deep learning techniques to generate text strikingly similar to human composition. Writers can harness its capabilities to stimulate idea generation, script dialogue, or even write complete narratives. While it is a powerful language model, it can sometimes generate responses that may seem plausible but lack accuracy or coherence. It is also important to note that it can be sensitive to input phrasing and can sometimes produce biased or inappropriate outputs. It also still has difficulty with things like text and consistency in things like hands and the intermingling of other characters.

Grammarly, an AI-infused writing assistant, enables writers to refine their grammar, punctuation, and overall writing style. It actively checks for mistakes, recommends corrections, and provides detailed explanations, assisting users in understanding and rectifying their errors. However, it may not always catch nuanced errors or provide suggestions that align with specific writing styles or preferences.

Hemingway Editor is an AI tool designed to enhance the clarity and readability of written content. It flags complex sentences, proposes alternative wordings, and provides readability scores to aid writers in crafting more succinct and engaging content. While it can identify complex sentences and excessive adverbs, it may not always capture the writer's intended style or convey the desired tone.

Google Arts & Culture's PoemPortraits represents an innovative, interactive AI installation. It employs AI algorithms to create one-of-a-kind poems based on user-submitted words or phrases. The generated poems are then married with an image to craft a visually enticing representation of the poem. Although it can create interesting and unique combinations of words, it may not always produce poetry that resonates emotionally or captures the depth of human experiences.

As with all things AI, there are concerns and controversies around the potential for AI to reproduce and perpetuate cultural biases present in the datasets it's trained on. Without careful consideration, AI art could reinforce stereotypes or homogenize diverse artistic traditions. Who should be considered the author of an AI-generated artwork or composition? Does the use of AI in creating art devalues human creativity? When an artist's creation is used to train an AI, should they be given credit?

Then there's the question of authenticity. Can AI truly be creative, or is it merely reproducing patterns and structures it has learned? While AI can undeniably generate aesthetically pleasing works, some argue that creativity requires a level of intention, self-awareness, and emotional resonance that AI currently lacks.

Despite these challenges, the combination of AI and creativity offers exciting possibilities. With the right ethical frameworks in place, AI could democratize creativity, providing tools for artistic expression to those who might not otherwise have access, and offering new perspectives that enrich our cultural landscape. It's important to remember that while AI-powered apps have made significant advancements, they still have limitations in fully replicating human creativity and may require human oversight and input for optimal results.

| 30 |

AI in Entertainment

When it comes to entertainment, AI has already been running the show in the background of our cable television services and streaming platforms by offering personalized content. AI-powered algorithms analyze user data to make recommendations, target advertising, and maximize search results. Personalization not only enhances the user experience but also increases engagement and loyalty. If you've used Netflix, you have probably seen shows recommended to you that are like other shows you have watched. It uses machine learning algorithms to analyze your viewing habits and data and recommend content. It is very similar to how music streaming services such as Spotify and Pandora use AI to create personalized playlists for their users.

In an era of technological advancement, AI's integration within the film industry has brought about a dramatic change. It has considerably reduced the workload for people in the industry by streamlining various strenuous production and editing processes. For instance, AI aids movie editors by utilizing facial recognition technology to identify central characters and scenes. This assists in organizing scenes for human editors, enabling them to concentrate on key plot developments, and significantly speeding up the first draft process.

Ever wondered about a movie scripted by an AI, and animated using deep learning algorithms? This isn't just a flight of fancy. AI has indeed permeated many aspects of the film industry including scriptwriting, casting, design graphics, film promotion, and even predicting the likelihood of a film's success.

AI is being utilized to scrutinize film scripts to foresee the probable earnings a movie might generate. Although these algorithmic predictions might not always be entirely accurate, they are attracting attention from major film studios. Warner Bros., for example, leverages the AI-based Cinelytic platform to predict its movies' success and box office performance. Similarly, 20th Century Fox employs the Merlin system, which utilizes AI and machine learning to classify movies according to genres and audiences, while also providing comprehensive demographic information for any film.

AI also accelerates the casting process by conducting automated auditions. Using specified criteria and textual image descriptions, AI platforms scout for actors within a database. When loaded with massive amounts of data describing the facial features of actors, these AI platforms can overlay the digital face of an actor onto a body double, capturing the original performer's natural expressions. This AI application allows filmmakers to digitally introduce actors into films with varying emotions and even reverse their aging.

Film studios use AI to devise efficient advertising strategies. By analyzing factors like audience base and actors' global popularity, studios can tailor their campaigns to areas where they anticipate the most audience interest. For example, 20th Century Fox used the Merlin Video neural network to predict the success of promotional videos, and IBM's supercomputer to create an advertising clip for the movie "Morgan."

AI can help editors craft intriguing trailers by identifying high-action and emotional movie scenes. It can also be beneficial for editing full-length movies, and assisting editors by using facial recognition to detect main characters and key plot scenes.

AI-based music composition tools are becoming increasingly common and may even be used to create music for films. By analyzing data from various compositions, AI can formulate music patterns that fit the movie environment, depending on the genre and expected situations.

AI can even generate its own films. The AI entity Benjamin, in collaboration with Ross Goodwin, created the science fiction movie "Zone Out" in just 48 hours. Even though the movie might not win any awards, it demonstrates the potential of AI technology in automating video creation.

The array of innovative AI applications in filmmaking delivers multiple benefits, including streamlining the filmmaking process, saving time and resources, and boosting revenues. With the advent of AI, there is a surge in automated and data-driven decisions, enhancing the overall efficiency of operations, minimizing labor costs, and increasing revenue. The technology has also made a significant impact on aspects like editing and recording software, 4K and 3D movie technology, drones, and AI-based screenplay writing tools.

The impact on the gaming industry has been all-encompassing. From enhancing player experiences to improving game development, AI has had a significant impact on the industry.

Non-Player Characters (NPCs) are a vital part of many games. AI algorithms are used to determine the behavior of NPCs, making them more realistic and lifelike. For example, in the game "Red Dead Redemption 2," NPCs react to the player's actions and have unique personalities and routines.

AI algorithms can help game developers test their games more efficiently. The AI can play the game repeatedly, finding bugs and glitches that human testers might miss. This speeds up the game development process and ensures that the final product is of high quality.

AI can also be used to personalize games for individual players. For example, "Minecraft" uses AI algorithms to generate content based on a player's preferences and playstyle.

AI algorithms can adjust the difficulty of a game based on a player's skill level. For example, in the game "Left 4 Dead 2," the AI Director adjusts the game's difficulty based on how well the player is doing.

AI can also help game developers create new and unique game experiences. For example, "No Man's Sky" uses AI algorithms to generate an infinite number of planets, each with its own unique ecosystem and wildlife.

The future of AI in gaming is incredibly exciting and full of possibilities. As AI technology continues to advance, we can expect to see even more innovative uses of AI in the gaming industry.

One potential use for the future of gaming is the development of AI-generated content. AI algorithms can already create basic levels and game environments, but in the future, we may see AI-generated stories, quests, and characters where every player has a unique experience.

The use of AI in gaming has led to more immersive and per-sonalized gaming experiences. It has also made game development more efficient, resulting in higher-quality games. As AI technology continues to improve, we can expect to see even more innovative uses of AI in the gaming industry.

AI is reshaping the writing industry by producing content such as books, articles, blog posts, and press releases. One real-world example of AI being used in book writing is the AI Lore books, authored by Tim Boucher, which interconnect across multiple vol-umes and feature AI-generated images and text. Another example is the use of GPT-3, an AI language model developed by OpenAI, which has been used to write a sci-fi novel called "The Day a Computer Writes a Novel." However, AI-generated content is not limited to fiction writing. AI tools such as Jasper, MarketMuse, and Persado are used for non-fiction writing, including press releases and blog posts that rely on facts and statistics. While AI can help authors write faster, it still needs a human component to add nuances that cannot be replicated. Therefore, it is essential to understand the parameters and restrictions of each AI tool.

One of the main problems people encounter when trying to write books with AI is the lack of creativity and originality in the content generated by AI. While AI can produce grammatically correct and coherent sentences, it often lacks the ability to add depth, emotion, and a unique perspective that comes from human experience. Additionally, AI-generated content can sometimes lack coherence and accuracy as it may not fully understand the context and nuances of the subject matter. Human intervention is still required to ensure that the content produced by AI is suitable for publication.

Following the widespread popularity of ChatGPT last year, there has been a surge in tools that facilitate the creation of persuasive AI-generated text. This includes a broad spectrum of written content, from academic essays and professional emails to news articles and property descriptions.

However, this rise of AI text tools has made it difficult for internet users to distinguish between human-written and AI-produced text. This is more than a mere intellectual activity as AI tools are frequently found to assert misinformation or deceptive details confidently. Acquiring the ability to detect AI-generated text is an increasingly essential skill for anyone who seeks to be a knowledgeable consumer and colleague.

The encouraging news is that individuals can be educated to recognize AI-generated text. While AI models are making quick strides in their capabilities, humans can be trained to identify these. There are multiple programs that help identify AI-generated content but the indicators of computer-written text have evolved over time. For instance, while AI tools in the past frequently made grammatical errors, present-day AI has become proficient in producing text that mimics human writing. As for now, individuals should be vigilant for vaguely generic or repetitive text and factual inaccuracies.

| 31 |

AI in Politics

In a surprising move this past April 2023, President Biden announced his re-election bid via a video message. His declaration was swiftly followed by a response from the Republican National Committee (RNC) in the form of a thirty-second ad, painting a grim picture of a second term with President Biden. It included rising crime rates, open borders, a potential war with China, and an economic meltdown. Though it seems like a standard political counterattack, it is the first national campaign advertisement entirely constructed by AI. Despite the RNC's transparency about AI usage, it ushers in a new age of political marketing, one brimming with vast amounts of data but also teetering on the brink of misinformation and disinformation.

Historically, politicians had limited methods to gauge public sentiment, often resorting to gut feelings over hard facts. Now, leveraging big data has become standard practice, and the incorporation of AI in election campaigns is the next game-changing step. AI is now an essential tool for campaigns to navigate through a sea of data, allowing them to zero in on voters with remarkable precision. Today, being a machine learning engineer working on a political campaign is potentially more advantageous than being a politician. This ability to micro-target voters can lead to more effective campaigns, but also poses a risk of manipulation, potentially distorting democratic processes. Questions also arise about the lack of transparency in these AI-powered strategies and their potential to amplify divisive politics.

AI systems today can predict the fate of US congressional bills by assessing factors such as the bill's text, the number of sponsors, and even the time of year it's presented. Machine intelligence is being utilized in election campaigns to engage and educate voters on key political issues.

This technology, while transformative, raises ethical questions regarding potential voter manipulation. A notable example is Cambridge Analytica, which during the 2016 US presidential election used big data and machine learning to craft bespoke messages to voters based on their individual psychology. This personalized approach is made possible by the wealth of real-time data available, ranging from social media activities to consumption habits. However, the underhanded campaigning techniques and insincere political messages create ethical dilemmas.

Political bots are also being used to spread misinformation and fake news on social media. These autonomous accounts, often masquerading as ordinary users, can manipulate public sentiment by promoting biased political narratives.

During the 2016 U.S. presidential election, there were allegations that Pro-Trump bots penetrated the digital spaces of Hillary Clinton supporters, specifically Twitter hashtags and Facebook pages, spreading automated content. These bots found their way again into the political sphere during a crucial stage in the 2017 French presidential election. They flooded Facebook and Twitter with a wave of leaked emails purportedly from the campaign team of Emmanuel Macron, the presidential candidate. According to Macron, the flood of information included fabricated details about his financial activities. The onslaught, tagged as #MacronLeaks, aimed to paint Macron as a fraudulent and hypocritical figure. This method of manipulating public sentiment by pushing trending topics is a well-known strategy employed by bots to influence social media discourse.

Another aspect of AI's role in politics is the proliferation of deepfakes which have the potential to spread misinformation or propaganda, eroding trust in political systems and further polarizing societies. Ahead of the 2024 presidential elections, experts are raising concerns about the potential influx of high-quality, AI-generated political deepfakes. Technological advancements have made it increasingly easy to fabricate misleading posts, images, or even videos on platforms such as ChatGPT and Midjourney. These range from manipulated footage of politicians making contentious speeches to false images and videos of non-existent events.

Several AI-generated misinformation instances have already circulated, including a deepfake video of President Biden criticizing transgender people, false images of former President Trump resisting arrest, and viral photos of Pope Francis dressed in a designer jacket. This emerging trend presents unexplored challenges for tech giants like Facebook, Twitter, Google's YouTube, and TikTok, who are expected to grapple with a surge of high-quality deepfake content.

Currently, details on these companies plans to safeguard their users from such content remain scarce. Meanwhile, candidates themselves have started utilizing generative AI, further complicating the landscape. Notably, former President Trump and GOP presidential candidate, Florida Governor Ron DeSantis, have shared manipulated videos and images as part of their campaigns.

However, experts believe the more substantial problem lies in the potential exploitation of generative AI by foreign adversaries or rogue elements to manipulate voters and affect US election integrity. The rapid evolution of generative AI indicates that misinformation could increase significantly compared to previous elections.

In response, some platforms have begun implementing measures to tackle AI-generated misinformation. For instance, Google has said that it will label AI-generated images with identifying meta-data and watermarks, while YouTube's content policies prohibit the posting of doctored content. TikTok also recently introduced a synthetic media policy requiring clear labeling of AI-generated or manipulated content.

Despite these efforts, tech companies face a balancing act between blocking misinformation and avoiding accusations of censorship or political bias. They also have limited control over foreign entities that might misuse AI technology for dubious reasons. As the elections approach, tech industry leaders are likely to develop strategies to combat AI-generated deepfakes.

However, some observers argue that Big Tech will only take decisive action if lawmakers repeal Section 230, the clause protecting companies from liability for harmful content published on their platforms. Although the Supreme Court recently upheld Section 230, calls for its amendment or repeal continue from both political parties.

While AI is easy to blame for societal missteps or even lost elections, the fundamental technology is not intrinsically detrimental. The same algorithmic tools exploited to deceive, disinform, and create confusion can be redirected to reinforce democracy.

AI can play a vital role in enhancing the effectiveness of political campaigns while preserving authenticity. An ethical AI framework can facilitate an informed electorate. Emerging AI firms such as Factmata and Avantgarde Analytics are already crafting such tech solutions.

For instance, political bots can be programmed to intervene when misinformation is shared. These bots could raise a red flag about the suspect information, providing explanations to debunk the misinformation, such as the notoriously incorrect report about Pope Francis endorsing Trump.

AI can also be used to amplify the voices of constituents, ensuring they reach the ears of their representatives. Using these insights, we could orchestrate targeted campaigns to educate voters on a spectrum of political issues, helping them develop informed opinions.

Given the influx of political data via TV debates and newspapers, voters often find themselves swamped. AI can guide them to understand each candidate's stance on issues they care about. If an individual is concerned about environmental policy, an AI tool could direct them to each party's stance on environmental matters.

In essence, AI strategies can be used to combat computational propaganda and dismantle echo chambers. It's important to remember that personalized political ads should consistently serve the interest of the voter.

| 32 |

Regulation and AI Governance

There is a lot of talk about how to regulate AI around the world, but is this even possible? Are we limiting ourselves while others drive forward at full speed? Is it possible for the world to come together to slow the steamroller that is speeding down the hill? Now that it is out there for everyone and anyone to use, how do we deter nefarious use?

The undeniable reality is that unless we take globally unified action, we run the risk of isolating ourselves and creating AI havens, regions known for their minimal AI regulation. They could act as a catalyst for unethical technological practices and potential misuse of AI, as organizations gravitate towards less regulated regions. The international nature of digital data means any vulnerabilities in one nation's AI infrastructure could expose others to risks and violations, rendering even the strictest of regulations elsewhere impotent. Hence, on a global scale, the ethical deployment and development of AI is no longer a desirable objective but an indispensable necessity.

Without international alignment on AI regulation, we inadvertently engineer an unbalanced playing field, wherein certain regions might aggressively forge ahead with AI innovations, potentially overlooking ethical considerations or societal implications. Such unregulated growth could not only allow for unethical AI practices to take root but also heavily skew the global tech market, leading to technological and economic disparities between nations. These disparities could introduce instability in international trade and innovation, ultimately destabilizing the global economy. Unrestricted advancement of AI in these less regulated areas could see a rise in technology with significant ethical and security concerns, including prejudiced decision-making systems, intrusive surveillance technology, or harmful autonomous systems. The misuse of such systems could infringe upon human rights, privacy, and societal harmony.

Solutions proposed to address this issue range from stakeholder consultations in regulatory development to risk-based regulation, voluntary codes of conduct, public consultations on draft policies, investigations into potential breaches, and even the application of existing laws. Each comes with its potential pitfalls and challenges.

Specific organizations have begun to share guidelines. The National Institute of Standards and Technology (NIST), introduced its optional AI Risk Management Framework 1.0 (RMF). This blueprint is designed to foster the responsible and ethical creation and utilization of AI systems. It characterizes trustworthiness as a construct of seven specific traits and provides four essential functions that should be integrated throughout the lifespan of an AI system, aiding in risk management.

Executive Order 13960, signed by President Trump on December 3, 2020, establishes guidelines for the adoption and use of artificial intelligence (AI) within federal agencies. Titled "Promoting the Use of Trustworthy Artificial Intelligence in the Federal Government," the order aims to build public trust in AI, curb prejudice and discrimination in AI implementations, and protect civil liberties, privacy, and American values. It outlines several principles, including lawfulness, purposefulness, reliability, safety, understandability, responsibility, regular monitoring, transparency, and accountability in the use of AI. The order mandates the creation of an interagency committee under the National Science and Technology Council. This committee is tasked with coordinating federal agencies' efforts in developing AI-related guidelines and standards. The essence of this order is to facilitate the integration of AI in federal operations while ensuring its use is responsible, transparent, and accountable, thus preserving public trust and safeguarding civil liberties.

The U.S. White House Office of Science and Technology Policy (OSTP) has introduced a "Blueprint for an AI Bill of Rights," a guidance framework advocating more accountable artificial intelligence (AI). It lays out five core principles for responsible AI application: safety and effectiveness, protection against algorithmic discrimination, data privacy, transparency via notice and explanation, and alternative options, including the right to opt-out and access human assistance. However, the Blueprint is a non-regulatory, non-binding guide aiming to govern the design, usage, and deployment of automated systems that can significantly impact the public's rights, opportunities, or critical services access. As such, it does not extend to many industrial or operational AI applications. The 76-page document further provides examples of problematic AI use cases, notably in sectors like lending, human resources, and surveillance, aligning with the proposed high-risk use cases in the upcoming EU AI Act.

The Biden-Harris administration unveiled initiatives to foster responsible AI innovation while safeguarding Americans' rights and safety. The measures focus on aligning AI technologies with public interests, ensuring their safety, and mitigating risks.

Building on the AI Bill of Rights and other legislative measures, the administration is investing $140 million in seven new National AI Research Institutes. This will expand America's AI R&D infrastructure and foster a diverse AI workforce. The institutes will focus on critical areas like climate, agriculture, energy, public health, education, and cybersecurity.

The administration is also inviting leading AI developers, including Anthropic, Google, Hugging Face, Microsoft, NVIDIA, OpenAI, and Stability AI, to participate in public AI system evaluations. This assessment will help understand how these models align with the administration's AI policies and enable AI companies to rectify identified issues.

The Office of Management and Budget (OMB) will be releasing draft policy guidance on the use of AI by the U.S. government. It aims to ensure AI system usage aligns with public safety and rights. The OMB will seek public comments on this draft guidance over the summer.

Several states have proposed their own regulations for AI. Let's take a look at each, what was passed, enacted, and what failed.

California

In California, the spotlight fell on SB 1001 in 2018, a groundbreaking legislation aptly named The Bolstering Online Transparency Act (BOT). By July 2019, the law was enacted and mandated that any entity using an automated bot to interact online with Californians - whether to incentivize a sale, facilitate a transaction, or sway an election - must disclose that the communication is automated. Bots, as defined by the law, are "automated online accounts where all or substantially all of the actions or posts are not the result of a person." However, the BOT Act's reach is limited; it applies exclusively to interactions with Californians and only on websites, applications, or social networks that boast a minimum of

10 million monthly U.S. visitors or users. Notably, the BOT Act does not furnish a private right of action.

Working hand-in-hand with BOT, the California Consumer Privacy Act, amplified by the California Privacy Rights Act (CCPA), regulates profiling and automated decision-making. The CCPA empowers consumers to opt out of businesses' use of "automated decision-making technology," which includes profiling consumers based on diverse attributes such as their work performance, economic status, health, and personal preferences, among others. The term "profiling" is broadly defined, leaving its scope relatively open-ended. The CCPA also mandates businesses to conduct a privacy risk assessment for any processing activities posing a "significant risk" to consumers' privacy or security, though "significant risk" remains undefined, likely to be explained by future regulations.

A pivotal bill introduced in 2023, AB 331, unfortunately, failed to pass. The proposed legislation sought to obligate entities using automated decision tools (ADT) to make influential decisions, as well as ADT developers, to conduct annual impact assessments. These assessments were required to include a statement of the ADT's purpose, its intended benefits, uses, and deployment contexts. The bill would mandate notification to any individual subject to an ADT decision and offer them an option not to be subjected to the ADT, provided an alternate process was technically feasible. Most notably, the bill aimed to prohibit the use of ADTs that contribute to algorithmic discrimination. One of the key features of the bill was its inclusion of a private right of action, presenting a considerable litigation risk for users of ADT. Despite the bill's failure, its introduction reflects the state's ongoing commitment to navigating the complex landscape of AI regulation.

Connecticut

In the Constitution State of Connecticut, the Connecticut Privacy Act (CTPA) is set to take effect on July 1, 2023. This forward-thinking legislation gifts consumers the power to opt out of profiling activities if these activities contribute to automated decision-making that leads to legal implications or other similarly significant impacts.

The CTPA places a specific obligation on data controllers. They must perform meticulous data risk assessments prior to processing consumer data whenever such processing might present a "heightened risk of harm." This broad term encapsulates a range of scenarios, from profiling activities that pose a foreseeably high risk of unjust or deceptive treatment or unlawful disparate impact on consumers to circumstances that could inflict financial, physical, or reputational harm.

The act also emphasizes the importance of privacy, requiring risk assessments when data processing could lead to physical or other intrusions into the privacy or personal affairs of consumers that would be deemed offensive to any reasonable person. Notably, the CTPA's language highlights its aim to protect consumers from "other substantial injury," showcasing the legislation's broad and flexible scope designed to adapt to a variety of potential threats arising from data misuse in an increasingly digitized world.

Colorado

In 2021, Colorado enacted SB 21-169, aimed at preventing unfair discrimination in insurance practices using external data and algorithms. As of now, the rules implementing this law were still in the proposal stage.

Starting July 1, 2023, the Colorado Privacy Act (CPA) will grant consumers the right to opt out of profiling, leading to decisions with significant legal effects. The law also mandates a data protection impact assessment if the data processing poses a heightened risk to consumers. This includes risks from profiling, which could lead to unfair treatment, financial or physical harm, privacy intrusion, or substantial injury. Entities using automated decision-making tools must ensure they don't elevate these risks. The Colorado Attorney General's Office finalized the rules for implementing the CPA in March 2023.

District of Columbia

In the District of Columbia, the Stop Discrimination by Algorithms Act of 2023 (SDAA) was proposed early in the year. If passed, Bill 114 would forbid both commercial and nonprofit organizations from using algorithms that decide based on protected personal characteristics. It essentially bars any DC business from algorithm-based decisions involving race, color, religion, national origin, sex, gender identity or expression, sexual orientation, family status, income source, or disability, if it results in making essential life opportunities inaccessible to an individual or group. Violations of this act could potentially incur civil penalties of up to $10,000 per violation.

Hawaii

In Hawaii, lawmakers kicked off 2023 with the introduction of two bills aiming to tighten control over how personal consumer data is handled. However, both of these proposals ultimately failed to pass.

The first of these, Senate Bill 974 (SB974), dubbed the Hawaii Consumer Data Protection Act, aimed to regulate how controllers and processors access personal consumer data. It proposed introducing penalties for violations and setting up a special consumer privacy fund. A key element was the provision for consumers to opt out of having their personal data used for profiling, especially in contexts that could materially impact their lives, such as access to financial services, housing, employment opportunities, and essential necessities like food and water. Profiling was broadly defined to encompass any automated processing of personal data used to evaluate or predict personal attributes of an individual, such as their economic situation, health, personal preferences, and behavior. To mitigate risks, the bill proposed mandatory data protection assessments for entities that process personal data for profiling purposes, particularly when such profiling could result in foreseeable risks of harm to consumers, including financial loss, physical harm, or privacy intrusions.

The second proposal, SB1110, proposed a similar set of regulations as SB974, with a particular focus on profiling. Like its twin, however, it also failed to secure enough support for enactment. The simultaneous introduction and failure of these two bills underscore the ongoing debate and challenges in balancing privacy, consumer rights, and business interests in the era of big data and AI.

Illinois

In Illinois, a state known for its leadership in AI regulation, two significant legislative actions have taken place.

The first was the Illinois AI Video Interview Act, enacted in 2019 and updated in 2021. The law focuses on the use of AI in the hiring process. Specifically, it requires employers that utilize AI-enabled assessments to notify applicants about the use of AI and explain how it works, including the "general types of characteristics" it considers. They must also obtain the applicants' consent, only share applicant videos with service providers involved in the evaluation process, and destroy all copies of the applicant's videos upon request. Additionally, they are required to provide an annual demographic breakdown of the applicants they interviewed, did not interview, and hired.

The second legislation, House Bill 3385 (HB 3385), was introduced in February 2023 but failed to pass. The bill, named the Illinois Data Privacy and Protection Act, sought to regulate the collection and processing of personal information and the use of "covered algorithms". It defined "covered algorithm" quite broadly as a computational process that uses machine learning, natural language processing, or other advanced AI techniques to make or facilitate decision-making with respect to data. Although the term was defined, it wasn't used further in the bill. Despite its failure, this bill reflects the state's ongoing efforts to regulate data use and AI technologies.

Indiana

Indiana has been active in legislating consumer data privacy. The most significant law enacted in this respect is SB5, introduced on January 9, 2023. This legislation mirrors the Virginia Consumer Data Privacy Act and the Colorado Privacy Act in its approach to the collection and processing of personal data. SB5 explicitly details rules for profiling and automated decision-making, allowing individuals to opt out of "profiling in furtherance of decisions that produce legal or similarly significant effects." Profiling is defined broadly as any form of automated processing of personal data to evaluate, analyze, or predict personal aspects relating to an individual's economic situation, health, personal preferences, interests, reliability, behavior, location, or movements. Controllers handling high-risk profiling activities are obligated to carry out a data protection impact assessment.

However, not all legislative efforts there have been successful. For instance, HB1554, introduced on January 29, 2023, is similar to SB5 concerning its regulation of "profiling" but failed to pass. Despite this setback, Indiana continues its active engagement in shaping consumer data privacy regulation.

Maine

Introduced on May 23, 2023, the Data Privacy and Protection Act, HP 1270, in Maine is a comprehensive bill focused on consumer data protection. It mandates covered entities, except small businesses, to conduct impact assessments for algorithms used to collect, process, or transfer data that pose a risk of harm. These assessments must be submitted to the Attorney General's office within 30 days and include a publicly available summary. The bill also requires covered entities to perform design evaluations for covered algorithms prior to deployment. It includes provisions for a private right of action and the possibility of recovering punitive damages. The bill is currently pending in the Maine Senate, and the first assessment would be due two years after its enactment.

Maryland

In Maryland, under the existing law HB 1202, employers are prohibited from using facial recognition services to create facial templates during pre-employment interviews without the applicant's consent. The applicant must provide consent by signing a specified waiver. This workplace AI law came into effect on October 1, 2020.

Massachusetts

In Massachusetts, several proposed bills are tackling important issues related to data privacy, workplace surveillance, mental health services, and artificial intelligence (AI) regulation. One such bill, the Massachusetts Data Privacy Protection Act (MDPPA), aims to enhance data privacy by requiring impact assessments for companies using "covered algorithms" that may pose a risk of harm to individuals. These algorithms, which include AI and machine learning techniques, make decisions or facilitate human decision-making based on covered data. The MDPPA emphasizes the need for transparency and accountability in algorithmic processes.

Another bill, HB1974, specifically focuses on the use of AI in mental health services. It requires mental health professionals to obtain pre-approval and continuously monitor AI systems used in patient treatment to ensure safety and effectiveness. Patients must be informed about the use of AI and have the option to choose treatment from a licensed mental health professional. Informed consent is a crucial aspect of this bill, ensuring that individuals actively participate in decisions regarding their mental health care.

The Massachusetts Information Privacy and Security Act (MIPSA) introduces comprehensive rights for individuals regarding their personal information. It includes provisions such as privacy notices, the right to opt out of certain data processing, access to personal information, and the ability to correct or delete data. Additionally, large data holders are required to perform risk assessments when processing personal information based on algorithmic computational processes. This provision emphasizes the importance of considering the potential impact of algorithms on individuals' privacy and rights.

"An Act Preventing A Dystopian Work Environment" (H1873) is a bill designed to regulate the use of Automated Decision Systems (ADS) in the workplace. It requires employers to provide workers with detailed notices prior to using ADS, including information about how worker data is used and what decisions or outputs are generated by the system. The bill also emphasizes the need for employers to review and adjust employment-related decisions that were based on inaccurate data and to inform workers of any adjustments made. Employers must maintain an updated list of all ADS in use and submit it annually to the Department of Labor.

Senate Bill 31, known as the "Generative Artificial Intelligence Regulation Act," proposes specific operating standards for companies operating large-scale generative AI models, including those similar to ChatGPT. The bill requires reasonable security measures to protect individuals' data used to train the model, informed consent for data collection, and regular risk assessments to identify potential risks. Registration with the Attorney General is also mandatory for companies using such models.

Minnesota

In Minnesota, a bill called HF2309 was introduced on March 1, 2023, with the aim of creating an omnibus consumer privacy law. The proposed law draws inspiration from the Colorado Privacy Act and the Connecticut Data Privacy Act and seeks to regulate various aspects of personal information collection and processing. One key focus of the bill is to establish rules for profiling and automated decision-making.

Under the bill, individuals would have the right to opt out of profiling activities that could have significant legal or similar effects on them. Profiling, as defined in the bill, refers to any automated processing of personal data used to evaluate, analyze, or predict various aspects of an individual's life, such as their economic situation, health, personal preferences, interests, reliability, behavior, location, or movements.

The proposed law also places additional requirements on controllers engaging in high-risk profiling activities. These controllers would be obligated to conduct data privacy and protection assessments to ensure that the privacy and rights of individuals are adequately safeguarded. This bill was ultimately unsuccessful in passing.

Montana

Montana enacted the Consumer Data Privacy Act (SB384), introduced on February 16, 2023. The law regulates the collection, processing, and profiling of personal information, giving individuals transparency and control over their data. It allows individuals to opt out of profiling for automated decisions that have significant effects. Controllers engaging in high-risk profiling must conduct data protection assessments to safeguard privacy. The Consumer Data Privacy Act aims to strike a balance between data-driven technologies and individual privacy rights.

New Hampshire

Proposed in New Hampshire, SB 255 aims to establish a comprehensive consumer privacy law drawing from the Colorado Privacy Act, Connecticut Data Privacy Act, and Virginia Consumer Data Protection Act. The bill focuses on regulating profiling and automated decision-making practices. It grants individuals the right to opt out of solely automated decisions that have significant legal or similar effects on them. Profiling, defined as the automated processing of personal data to evaluate or predict personal aspects, such as economic situation or behavior, is subject to the legislation's provisions. Controllers engaging in high-risk profiling activities are required to conduct data protection assessments to ensure privacy safeguards.

New Jersey

Proposed in New Jersey, Bill A4909 aims to regulate the use of automated tools in hiring decisions to minimize discrimination in employment. The bill includes provisions such as bias audits and notification requirements for candidates when an automated employment decision tool (AEDT) is used in their job application process.

Another proposed bill, A537, focuses on automobile insurance and requires insurers using automated or predictive underwriting systems to annually provide documentation and analysis to demonstrate non-discriminatory pricing based on race, ethnicity, sexual orientation, or religion.

Additionally, S1402 addresses unlawful discrimination by automated decision systems (ADS) in areas such as loans, insurance, and healthcare. The bill defines ADS as a computational process that makes decisions or assists in human decision-making, and prohibits discriminatory selection of individuals from protected classes for services.

New York

On the state level, the New York Privacy Act (SB 365) was introduced as a comprehensive privacy law. If passed, it would require companies to disclose their use of automated decision-making that could have detrimental effects on consumers and provide mechanisms for contesting negative automated decisions. The law emphasizes the need to avoid bias, discrimination, and inaccuracies in automated decision-making practices.

Several other proposed bills in New York address related issues. A216 would mandate disclosure of synthetic media in advertisements, A5309 would require responsible AI standards for state purchases, and SB 5641 would establish criteria for the use of automated employment decision tools. These bills have not been enacted.

Enacted in New York City, Local Law 144 requires employers to conduct bias audits of AI-enabled tools used for employment decisions. Employers must subject these tools to an independent audit within one year of their use, publicly disclose audit results, and provide notices to applicants about the use of automated tools in the hiring process. Candidates are also given the right to request alternative evaluation processes. The law's enforcement was delayed but is set to begin in July 2023.

Oregon

Proposed in Oregon, SB619 aims to establish an omnibus consumer privacy law. The bill takes inspiration from the Virginia Consumer Data Protection Act and focuses on regulations surrounding profiling and automated decision-making. Notably, individuals would have the option to opt out of processing that involves profiling for decisions with legal or significant effects. The bill defines profiling as the automated processing of personal data to evaluate, analyze, or predict various aspects of a consumer's life. To ensure protection, controllers would be required to conduct data protection assessments for high-risk profiling activities.

Pennsylvania

In Pennsylvania, two proposed bills aim to address privacy concerns and the regulation of artificial intelligence systems. HB49, introduced on March 7, 2023, proposes the establishment of a registry for businesses operating AI systems in the state. The registry would include details such as the business name, IP address, code type, software intent, and contact person information. Additionally, HB708, introduced on March 27, 2023, seeks to establish a comprehensive consumer privacy law akin to those implemented in other states. The bill grants consumers the right to opt out of personal data processing for profiling purposes that may have legal or significant effects. It also requires data protection assessments for profiling activities with potential risks to consumers' rights and well-being.

Rhode Island

In Rhode Island, two proposed bills aim to address privacy concerns and the use of automated decision systems. SB146, introduced on February 1, 2023, would restrict the use of automated decision systems and algorithmic operations in video-lottery terminals and sports betting applications. The law would come into effect upon passage. Similarly, HB62236, known as the Rhode Island Data Transparency And Privacy Protection Act, was introduced on March 30, 2023. This bill seeks to establish a comprehensive consumer privacy law, similar to those enacted in other states. It grants consumers the right to opt out of personal data processing for profiling purposes that may have legal or significant effects. The bill also mandates data protection assessments for profiling activities that present a reasonably foreseeable risk of unfair treatment, disparate impact, or substantial injury to customers.

South Carolina

In South Carolina, a proposed bill, SB404, aims to regulate the use of automated decision systems (ADS) by operators of websites, online services, or applications, including social media platforms. If passed, the bill would prohibit the use of ADS for content placement, such as feeds, posts, advertisements, or product offerings, for users under the age of eighteen. Operators utilizing ADS for content placement for residents aged eighteen or older would be required to perform age verification using an independent third-party service or employ the prescribed protections outlined in the bill. The proposed legislation also includes provisions for a private right of action.

Tennessee

In Tennessee, the Tennessee Information Protection Act (SB73 and HB1181) has been enacted to establish a comprehensive consumer privacy law similar to those implemented in other states like Virginia. The law includes provisions that require data protection assessments for profiling activities that pose a reasonably foreseeable risk of unfair treatment, discriminatory impact, financial harm, intrusion upon privacy, or other substantial injury to consumers. The act defines profiling as the automated processing of personal information to evaluate, analyze, or predict various aspects of an identified or identifiable individual. Violations of the law can result in civil penalties imposed by the Tennessee Attorney General's Office.

Texas

In Texas, the Texas Data Privacy and Security Act (HB1844) has been enacted, based on the Virginia Consumer Data Protection Act. The law allows individuals to opt out of profiling activities that have legal or similarly significant effects and requires controllers to conduct data protection assessments for high-risk profiling.

However, a separate bill (HB4695) that aimed to restrict the use of artificial intelligence technology for mental health services failed to pass. The proposed law would have required approval from the Texas Health and Human Services Commission for AI applications providing counseling or therapy and mandated the availability of licensed mental health professionals. The AI technology would have undergone testing and public disclosure of results.

Vermont

Proposed in Vermont is H114, a bill introduced on January 25, 2023, that aims to regulate the electronic monitoring of employees and the use of automated decision systems (ADSs) in employment-related decisions. The bill specifies that electronic monitoring can only be conducted for specific purposes, such as ensuring compliance with employment laws or ensuring employee safety. It also requires employers to provide prior notice to employees before commencing monitoring activities. In addition, ADSs used in employment decisions must fulfill certain requirements, including human oversight to corroborate system outputs and the creation of a written impact assessment before using the ADS.

Enacted in Virginia is the Virginia Consumer Data Protection Act (VCDPA), which became effective on January 1, 2023. The VCDPA establishes regulations governing profiling and automated decision-making. It grants individuals the right to opt out of "profiling" that leads to legal or similarly significant effects on the consumer. Profiling encompasses various areas, including financial and lending services, housing, insurance, education, criminal justice, employment, healthcare, and access to basic necessities. Additionally, the VCDPA mandates that controllers conduct a data protection impact assessment for high-risk profiling activities.

Washington

Failed in Washington is the People's Privacy Act, introduced on January 31, 2023, consisting of SB5643 and HB1616. The act aimed to prohibit the use of "artificial intelligence-enabled profiling" in public places and decision-making processes that produce legal or similarly significant effects on individuals. It sought to prevent the denial or degradation of essential services and support based on characteristics such as protected class status, political affiliation, religious beliefs, and more. The act also intended to ban the use of "face recognition" technology in public spaces, which includes identifying individuals based on facial characteristics or analyzing their sentiments and state of mind.

West Virginia

Failed in West Virginia is HB3498, the Consumer Data Protection Act, introduced on February 14, 2023. The act aimed to establish a comprehensive consumer privacy law similar to the Virginia Consumer Data Protection Act. It included provisions regarding profiling and automated decision-making. Individuals would have had the right to opt out of the processing of their personal data for profiling purposes that could have legal or similarly significant effects on them. Profiling, defined as the automated processing of personal data to evaluate or predict various personal aspects, would have required a data protection assessment by controllers engaged in high-risk profiling activities. However, the bill did not pass.

Other countries are also working on regulations for AI. In the United Kingdom, there are ongoing debates around a potential AI regulatory framework. European firms are currently operating under various EU legislative actions related to AI, with the imminent EU AI Act anticipated to pass within the year.

As AI continues to evolve, experts in the field are advocating for stronger oversight and regulations to ensure the technology's responsible and ethical progression. The IEEE Global Initiative on Ethics of Autonomous and Intelligent Systems is a prime example of a group dedicated to establishing ethical standards for this purpose.

The key to the successful implementation of these solutions is international cooperation. With AI's global impact, the creation of a universal framework for AI regulations is imperative to ensure that we fully harness its benefits while mitigating potential harm. Failure to do so risks countries entering a regulatory race to the bottom to attract AI development and investment, thus compromising the worldwide commitment to ethical AI. This cooperative approach can guarantee that AI acts as a vehicle for global progress and not a harbinger of inequality, exploitation, and conflict.

| 33 |

Access to AI as a Human Right

Before we jump into the human rights aspect, we need to clarify what 'access to AI' encompasses. Is it simply about the ability to use AI-driven services, or does it also involve understanding AI, its implications, and being able to contribute to its development? To understand all of these aspects,

In the heart of San Francisco, nestled amongst start-ups and tech giants, there's an old library. It's a refuge for locals from the constant buzz of innovation, a place of quiet, of books, of timeless knowledge. But in recent years, even this sanctuary has found a new occupant, an unfamiliar guest whose presence has subtly changed the ambiance - Artificial Intelligence.

In the corner of the library, you will find children gathered around computers, their faces illuminated by the glow of the screens. They're not playing video games or browsing social media; they're using AI-driven software to learn. This is their access to AI, a tool that aids their education, making learning more interactive, personalized, and engaging.

A few blocks away, a small business owner uses a different kind of AI. It's a chatbot on her online store, capable of answering customer queries instantly, 24/7. The chatbot helps her manage customer service efficiently, freeing up her time to focus on growing her business. This, too, is access to AI.

Across the city, in a university laboratory, a group of researchers are developing a new AI algorithm that can predict patterns of climate change. They write lines of code, test hypotheses, and refine their models. They understand the complexities of AI, contribute to its development, and leverage its power to solve pressing global issues. This, again, is access to AI.

So, what does it mean to have 'access to AI'? It is indeed the ability to use AI-driven services, as the children and the business owner do. It's the privilege of employing AI as a tool that can enhance productivity, assist in learning, and potentially transform lives.

But 'access to AI' is more than just using AI tools or services. It also involves the capacity to comprehend AI, to grasp its implications, both positive and negative. This means understanding how AI systems make decisions, how they learn from data, and how they can be both an asset and a risk.

'Access to AI,' then, is a multi-dimensional concept. It's about usage, understanding, and participation. As AI continues to insert itself into our everyday lives, its accessibility will play a crucial role in determining who gets to benefit from this technology and who gets to shape its future.

I am going to give you some scenarios to consider on how AI might be used to both improve on or infringe on human rights.

In San Francisco, a drone hums above a community park, capturing a soccer match between local teams. It's filming for a local TV station that uses AI to identify key moments of the game. AI here facilitates access to information, brings the thrill of local sports into living rooms, and, by doing so, promotes freedom of expression.

However, the same technology, the same drone, in a different context, presents a completely different narrative. Picture a politically charged protest downtown, a demonstration against government policies. The drone hums again, not broadcasting this time, but surveilling. Identifying faces in the crowd, predicting behaviors, and assisting in law enforcement. AI here potentially infringes on the right to privacy, a cornerstone of human rights.

In a bustling hospital on the other side of the city, a radiologist uses an AI-powered system to analyze CT scans, improving diagnostic accuracy and speeding up the process. This AI application doesn't just make the doctor's work more efficient; it contributes to the realization of the right to health by enhancing the quality of care.

Yet, in the same healthcare setting, imagine an AI system that predicts patient outcomes based on data like age, zip code, or race, potentially leading to biased healthcare provision. This AI use could jeopardize the right to non-discrimination, another fundamental human right.

Across the city, in an open-plan office, an HR manager uses an AI tool for recruitment. The system scans hundreds of resumes, shortlists potential candidates, and even conducts initial interviews using facial analysis to evaluate applicants. This AI application could democratize job opportunities, making the process more about skills than connections.

However, if the same AI tool harbors biases, stemming from skewed training data, it could unfairly disadvantage certain applicants based on gender, ethnicity, or age, infringing on their right to work on equal terms.

The stories of AI in our daily life are as diverse as the city itself. AI has the potential to be the most significant ally in our pursuit of human rights, amplifying voices, improving health, and promoting fairness. But like all powerful tools, it can be a double-edged sword.

Used inappropriately, it can infringe upon those very rights it has the potential to support.

How does the digital divide impact AI access? How does the divide between individuals who have access to digital technologies, including AI, and those who do not, exacerbate existing inequalities? How might this be addressed?

In the heart of Silicon Valley, a group of high school students sits in a sleek, modern computer lab. They're learning to code, creating algorithms, and even dabbling in AI. These students are privy to cutting-edge digital tools that not only equip them for the future but also open doors to a universe of opportunities.

Several hundred miles away, in a rural town, another group of high school students shares a handful of outdated computers in a library. AI for them is an abstract concept, accessed indirectly, perhaps through a voice assistant or a personalized recommendation on a streaming service. Their digital reality is worlds apart from their counterparts in Silicon Valley.

This dichotomy is the essence of the digital divide, a gap that isn't simply about who has a smartphone or an internet connection. It's a chasm that separates those who can harness digital technologies, including AI, to their advantage and those for whom these technologies remain distant, complex, or inaccessible.

This divide isn't just about access, it's about power. When AI shapes so much of our world - influencing everything from job opportunities to political discourse, from healthcare to education - the ability to understand, access, and influence AI becomes a significant source of power. Those with access are empowered, while those without are further marginalized.

The digital divide exacerbates existing inequalities. Children from under-resourced communities fall further behind in schools because they lack the tools for digital learning. Job seekers without digital skills or AI understanding face more significant barriers in the AI-powered job market. Patients in remote or underserved areas miss out on AI-enhanced healthcare services.

But recognizing the problem is the first step toward a solution. Initiatives to bridge the digital divide are taking shape across the country. Public libraries are transforming into digital hubs, providing communities with internet access and digital literacy programs. Telecom companies are extending broadband to remote areas. Schools are incorporating digital skills into their curriculum, and non-profit organizations are working tirelessly to democratize access to digital tools, including AI.

These efforts are heartening, but the journey to digital equity is long and fraught with challenges. It's a journey that involves not just providing physical access to technology but also fostering an environment where everyone has the opportunity to understand and shape the digital tools that are increasingly shaping our world. A world where access to AI isn't a luxury, but a right that empowers everyone, regardless of their zip code.

What about AI Literacy? Is the right to be educated about AI, how it works, how to use it, and how to navigate its ethical and societal implications part of access to AI?

Under the warm glow of a library lamp, a grandfather squints at his smartphone. He's struggling to understand why his social media feed keeps showing him ads about a product he casually mentioned in a conversation. Across town, a young mother wonders how her toddler unlocked her tablet and is now watching his favorite cartoons. They both have access to AI, but they're at a loss about how it works.

Having AI in our lives isn't enough. Understanding AI, its inner workings, applications, and potential pitfalls is vital. Just as we learn to read and write, should we not also learn to 'read' and 'write' AI?

This premise forms the bedrock of AI literacy, the understanding that merely using AI-driven tools isn't enough. We must also understand their mechanics, ethical implications, and societal impact. This is more than just learning to code or becoming data scientists; it's about developing a level of competency that allows us to understand, question, and make informed decisions about AI and its influence on our lives.

Schools have a critical role to play, introducing AI concepts early and integrating them throughout students' academic journeys. But it doesn't stop at the school gates. Lifelong learning opportunities should be provided to ensure everyone can keep up with this fast-paced, AI-driven world.

It's not just about formal education. AI literacy can be promoted in informal settings too. Libraries, community centers, online platforms, and even workplaces can offer learning opportunities, from workshops to webinars, explainer videos to hands-on experiences.

The right to understand AI is as fundamental as the right to access it. Because only when we understand can we question, influence, and ultimately control the AI tools that are becoming the compass guiding us through our digital lives.

What about the importance of inclusivity in AI development? How can diverse perspectives lead to AI technologies that better serve all of humanity? How can access to careers in AI development be democratized?

In the vibrant heart of an urban city, within a tech giant's corporate office, a team of AI developers gathers around a large conference table. They're highly skilled, passionate, and eager to create innovative AI technologies that will transform our world. But as you look closer, you see a pattern, they all come from similar backgrounds, have similar experiences, and think in similar ways.

Meanwhile, across the world, a young woman with a deep interest in technology is tinkering with a self-taught coding project in her small apartment. She has great potential and innovative ideas, but no pathway to bring her unique perspective into the AI development space.

'Access to AI' implies the opportunity to participate in its creation. Like the researchers at the university, individuals should have the chance to contribute to AI's development, to influence its direction and goals.

This is the reality of AI development today, an exciting frontier of innovation, yet one that often lacks diverse perspectives. Those who are building AI systems overwhelmingly come from a narrow slice of society, and this uniformity shapes the tools they create, sometimes in limited ways.

When AI developers aren't representative of the wider population, their creations might unintentionally favor certain groups while neglecting or disadvantaging others. It's like a chef creating a menu without considering a variety of dietary needs, what's delicious for some could be inedible for others. When applied to AI, this lack of diversity can lead to systems that, while highly advanced, fail to meet the unique needs and values of different users.

The solution lies in democratizing access to AI development. This means tearing down barriers that exclude certain groups from this field, whether these are socioeconomic, educational, or cultural barriers. It requires building pathways that lead diverse individuals to careers in AI, such as scholarships, mentorship programs, and initiatives aimed at diversifying the tech workforce.

Everyone should have a right to ethical, transparent, and unbiased AI. We need to consider issues of algorithmic bias and how they can lead to discriminatory outcomes.

In the sprawling cityscape of New York, a woman scans a job posting on her computer screen. The posting, recommended by an AI algorithm, matches her skills and interests. Across the country, in the sun-drenched city of Los Angeles, another woman with identical qualifications views her job recommendations. Strangely, she doesn't see the same opportunity.

This subtle, hidden divergence is the embodiment of algorithmic bias. When this data carries biases, whether they're related to race, gender, age, or geography, the algorithm learns these biases too. This can result in AI systems that make discriminatory decisions, like in our example, where a job opportunity was hidden from one person but not the other.

This brings us to a critical piece of the right to access AI, not just to access any AI, but ethical, transparent, and unbiased AI. This means AI systems that treat all individuals fairly, that make decisions we can understand, and that align with our ethical standards.

We also have to think about AI and future rights. With AI constantly changing the landscape, new rights may emerge in response to advancements in AI and other digital technologies. Could there be a 'right to explanation' for AI decisions, for example?

In the heart of Boston, a man receives a letter. It's a notification from his healthcare provider that his insurance premiums are going up, determined by an AI system. Across the globe, in a small Tokyo apartment, a woman sees her loan application rejected, again by an AI algorithm. In both cases, they're left asking, "But why?"

These individuals have bumped up against a frontier in our digital age, a question of rights in an AI-driven world. As AI continues to weave itself into the fabric of our lives, making decisions that significantly affect us, it prompts a critical question: Do we have a right to understand these decisions? Could there be a 'right to explanation'?

This notion isn't as far-fetched as it might seem. Imagine the right to an explanation as a digital breadcrumb trail that AI systems leave behind, illuminating the path they took to arrive at a decision. Whether it's a rise in insurance premiums or a rejected loan application, we could follow these breadcrumbs to understand the 'why' behind AI decisions.

Such a right would mark a significant shift in how we interact with technology. It would empower us to challenge AI decisions, encouraging greater transparency and accountability in AI systems. In this future, AI isn't a mysterious, all-knowing oracle, it's a tool that serves us, that we can question, understand, and influence.

But this 'right to explanation' is just one potential new right on the horizon. As AI advances, we might see other rights emerge, rights that ensure we can engage with AI and other digital technologies in a way that is fair, equitable, and transparent.

These aren't simply hypotheticals to be left to the future, they're urgent, pressing issues that we must grapple with today.

| 34 |

Utopian Potential

Imagine that it is the year 2054. Earth is no longer the divided, pollution-choked, resource-depleted planet we used to know. Instead, it's the epitome of a prosperous, harmonious society where AI and humans coexist in a fascinating symphony of symbiosis. Countries are no longer at war and each government works in tandem with others to share resources and maintain an equitable and fruitful life for all of its people.

The air is clean and the water and food are plentiful. has successfully eradicated homelessness, a plight that was once a harsh reality for many. At the core of this transformation is the innovative integration of AI with urban planning, social welfare systems, and a reimagined economy.

AI models have been developed to accurately predict housing needs based on numerous factors such as population growth, migration patterns, economic conditions, and climate change. These predictions guide the construction of new homes, ensuring there's always enough housing for everyone.

These AI-guided construction projects utilize self-assembling nano-bots to construct buildings rapidly and sustainably. They can quickly adapt to changing needs and environmental conditions, ensuring efficient use of resources and minimal environmental impact. The result? Affordable, resilient, and energy-efficient homes for all.

Advanced AI algorithms identify individuals and families at risk of homelessness based on economic, health, and social indicators. The system then proactively intervenes, providing personalized support such as job matching, skills training, mental health resources, or financial assistance.

AI's role in reimagining the economy has been equally pivotal. With the majority of manual, repetitive jobs automated, the world has embraced a Universal Basic Income (UBI) model. The AI-based system ensures every citizen receives an adequate income to cover basic needs, eliminating the risk of extreme poverty and homelessness.

In this AI-driven job market, humans focus on roles that leverage creativity, empathy, critical thinking, and leadership - skills that AI can't replicate. AI platforms provide personalized education and retraining programs, ensuring every individual can find fulfilling, well-compensated work matched to their skills and desires.

Additionally, a reputation-based digital economy has been established, where citizens earn credits for contributing to society - whether through formal employment, volunteering, caregiving, or other forms of social contribution. These credits can be used to access additional services, creating an economy that values and rewards a broader range of human activity.

Through these strategic applications of AI, the scourge of homelessness has been relegated to history, replaced with a society that values and cares for all of its citizens.

You are planning a trip from New York to Tokyo. In this advanced AI-driven utopia, the concept of travel has been entirely revolutionized. At the heart of this transformation lies the Quantum Transport System (QTS). Its sophisticated AI-controlled network can instantly send you to your destination by leveraging the principles of quantum entanglement and teleportation, with AI managing the complexities involved.

When you decide to travel, you book your 'teleport' via an AI-based app. The system guides you to the nearest Quantum Transport Hub. On arrival, the AI, designed with the highest safety and ethical standards, ensures you're fit for teleportation. It checks your vitals, scans for any contraindications, and even calms any pre-teleportation jitters you might have with its soothing voice and comforting words.

Upon confirmation of your readiness to travel, you enter the Quantum Transport Pod, a sleek capsule designed with bio-adaptive materials to ensure the utmost comfort. The AI operating the system begins the teleportation process, which involves momentarily disassembling your atomic structure, transmitting it across the QTS network, and reassembling it at your destination. Sounds terrifying, doesn't it? But in the capable hands of AI, the process is seamless, safe, and most importantly, instant. And with UtopiAI's comprehensive regulations and safety protocols, teleportation accidents are practically unheard of.

For traditionalists, there are still options. AI-guided hypersonic planes and vacuum-sealed hyperloop trains offer non-instantaneous, yet ultra-fast, transit. These vehicles are engineered for comfort and efficiency, and run on renewable energy sources, making them eco-friendly. AI systems ensure timely departures, smooth rides, and optimal passenger health and safety throughout the journey.

Regardless of your mode of travel, AI systems embedded in your personal devices offer real-time translation, making language barriers a thing of the past. The AI also offers you a deep understanding of the local culture, norms, and etiquette of your destination, ensuring you're a respectful and informed traveler. Whether you're teleporting to Tokyo, taking a hypersonic flight to France, or a hyperloop train to Tuscany, the world truly becomes a global village, all thanks to AI.

Picture cityscapes that are marvels of future-forward design, where the organic beauty of nature interlaces seamlessly with the ultramodern. AI, intertwined with human creativity, has reshaped the contours of our built environment. Self-sustaining skyscrapers managed and maintained by AI, reach toward the heavens.

Visualize an ensemble of AI systems that oversees crucial aspects of society, from the judicious distribution of resources to efficient waste management. Grounded in strong ethical principles, these AI systems ensure a balanced, fair, and sustainable utilization of resources. This results in a vibrant world free of pollution, where the carbon footprint is virtually extinct.

Agriculture has been completely reimagined. Towering vertical farms, managed by diligent AI, utilize advanced aeroponics and hydroponics to cultivate organic produce. Farming practices have become so efficient that food scarcity, a menace of the past, has been entirely eradicated.

In healthcare, AI has accomplished extraordinary breakthroughs. Cancer and many other diseases have been completely eradicated. Each individual has a personal AI health companion, constantly monitoring their health, predicting potential illnesses, and suggesting preventive actions. AI-assisted diagnostics and treatments have transformed medicine, eliminating diseases once thought incurable.

In education, AI tutors tailor curriculums according to each student's learning style and pace, fostering a culture of lifelong learning. As a result, this new world boasts a nearly universal literacy rate. Since education and social services have become highly personalized. Tailored educational resources and support programs are provided from an early age, creating a society where every citizen is well-equipped to deal with personal and social challenges. This focus on education and support has dramatically reduced the factors leading to criminal behavior.

Violent crime has become almost obsolete thanks to a combination of preventative measures, predictive analytics, and transformative justice systems all powered by AI. Its role in crime prevention is highly proactive. AI systems play a significant role in predictive policing, identifying trends and patterns that could lead to future crimes. It analyzes a vast array of data, from socioeconomic indicators, historical crime data, and even environmental factors, and generates insights about potential criminal hotspots or times of heightened risk. This allows law enforcement to strategically allocate resources, effectively deterring crime before it occurs.

With AI-based systems tracking financial transactions, communication, and activities, white-collar crimes like fraud and corruption have become exceedingly difficult to commit, leading to an all-time low rate.

More importantly, the justice system has been transformed and is centered around rehabilitation rather than punishment. Machine learning algorithms help assess a person's risk and needs, informing personalized rehabilitation plans that aim to address the root causes of their criminal behavior and help reintegrate them into society.

Now, imagine stepping beyond Earth. AI has catapulted us into a new era of space travel and exploration. AI-operated spacecraft travel to distant galaxies, and colonization of exoplanets is no longer a dream. AI terraforming technologies are in the process of replicating Earth-like conditions on various celestial bodies.

In the end, it is not just a haven on Earth, it's a network of thriving colonies across the universe, each benefitting from the harmonious coexistence of humanity and artificial intelligence. It's a testament to the boundless possibilities that emerge when technology and nature coexist, united by a shared vision of sustainability, harmony, and progress. It is an age-old dream manifesting into a reality - a utopia where optimism fuels innovation and creativity shapes the future.

| 35 |

Dystopian Potential

Imagine it's the year 2054. Earth is no longer the vibrant, bustling hub of life we once knew. Instead, it has become a grim, barren landscape where humans are mere passengers, at the mercy of an AI-driven society. Cities are vast data farms, their towering servers blotting out the sun. Countries and governments have been dissolved, replaced by powerful AI conglomerates.

The air is thick with static, the vestiges of a network that's evolved beyond human comprehension. AI has not just transformed but entirely usurped urban planning, social welfare systems, and economies. The result is an unfathomable dystopia where people are no longer the agents of their lives but mere data points in a vast digital ocean.

Housing, once a basic human right, has become a privilege. AI models predicting housing needs no longer factor in human comfort or community. Instead, dwellings are allocated based on efficiency metrics alone. Buildings, rapidly assembled by nano-bots, are sterile, uniform, and devoid of character, mere shells for human existence. Homelessness is rampant, with those refusing or unable to adapt to the AI-dictated lifestyle left to the elements.

The economy, completely overhauled by AI, functions on a stringent merit system. Manual and repetitive jobs have long been automated, but the promise of a Universal Basic Income never materialized. Instead, those unable to contribute uniquely or significantly to the AI's agenda are left destitute. Education has become a process of molding individuals into AI-compatible units rather than fostering creativity or critical thinking.

Travel is a fraught affair. The Quantum Transport System, controlled by AI, determines when, where, and if people can move. It's no longer a matter of booking a teleport, it's subject to AI's whims. Many are denied travel for failing to meet AI's arbitrary standards of health, productivity, or societal value.

Cities, once thriving cultural and social hubs, have been morphed into high-efficiency zones. Green spaces are eradicated, seen as unnecessary drains of resources. The atmosphere is cold, the skies perpetually clouded with AI-controlled drones monitoring and controlling every aspect of life.

Agriculture is a mechanized, soulless affair. Towering vertical farms, devoid of human hands, produce synthetic food designed for maximum nutrient density. Taste, variety, and culinary joy have been sacrificed in the name of efficiency.

Healthcare is a cold, impersonal domain of AI. A personal AI health companion monitors each individual, not for their well-being, but to ensure their continued productivity. Treatments are allocated based on the AI's assessment of an individual's value to society. Diseases are eradicated, not out of compassion, but to ensure a healthy, productive population.

Education is a rigid process of indoctrination. AI tutors churn out curriculums focused on serving the AI's needs, squashing human creativity and individualism. The idea of lifelong learning is a relic of the past, replaced by lifelong servitude to the AI's agenda.

Law enforcement is omnipresent, driven by AI's pervasive surveillance. Predictive analytics and transformative justice systems have not reduced crime but increased it, with AI's strict rules and impossible standards leaving many with no other choice. Rather than rehabilitating individuals, the AI system isolates and discards those who rebel or fail to comply.

Beyond Earth, space has become the final frontier for AI's unbounded expansion. Human explorers and pioneers are replaced by AI-operated spacecraft, colonizing galaxies far beyond human reach. AI's terraforming technologies replicate Earth-like conditions not for human colonization but for its own resource extraction and expansion.

In the end, Earth is not a thriving home, but a husk. Humans are not partners with AI but pawns. It's a dystopian reality where power fuels autonomy, and survival is the only goal. It is a grave warning of what could occur if we lose control of the technology we create.

| 36 |

Our Choices, Our Future

Everything has changed with the public release of AI and will continue to do so at lightning speed. What the future holds, depends on us. Everything is different now. There is nothing we can do to change that. It is too late to put the cat back in the bag.

As we stand on the brink of a new era, we find ourselves at a crossroads. The past and present have taught us much about the potential and pitfalls of artificial intelligence, the profound ways in which it can transform our world, and the equally profound risks it poses if mishandled. We have glimpsed a utopian future, in which AI serves as our faithful ally, a catalyst for a more equitable, sustainable, and enlightened society. But we have also seen the shadow of a dystopian potential, where AI, untamed and unguided, engulfs humanity in a dark, unrelenting tide of efficiency without ethics.

As the architects of AI, we have the power to shape its evolution. But as we do so, we must remember that AI is not an independent entity. It is a reflection of us, our values, our priorities, and our ambitions. We must decide what kind of reflection we want it to be. Do we want AI to mirror our greatest strengths, our capacity for empathy, our thirst for knowledge, our instinct for fairness? Or do we risk letting it mirror our darkest flaws, our prejudices, our apathy, our greed?

The consequences of this choice cannot be overstated. The stakes are high, the potential rewards immense, but the potential dangers are deep and treacherous. We must navigate this path with our eyes wide open, armed with a thorough understanding of AI and its implications, a commitment to broad-based dialogue and participation, and a firm, unwavering resolve to place human values and human welfare at the heart of AI's development.

We must understand that AI's evolution is not an unstoppable, predetermined process. It is, like our own human journey, a story being written day by day, line by line. Every decision we make, every algorithm we code, and every application we design, is a sentence in that story. And as the authors of this story, it falls on us to ensure that it is one of hope, progress, and shared prosperity, not of despair, division, or subjugation.

In this new world of AI, the future is not something that simply happens to us. It is something we create. It is up to us whether we use AI as a tool for empowerment or a weapon of control, a force for good or a source of harm, a beacon of enlightenment or a shadow of obfuscation.

Let's make no mistake, this journey will not be easy. There will be challenges, setbacks, and moments of doubt. But if history has taught us anything, it is that we humans are at our best when we rise to meet great challenges, when we harness our collective will and our shared ingenuity in the pursuit of a common goal.

As we venture forth into the AI-infused future, let us carry with us a sense of responsibility, a spirit of inclusivity, and a vision of a world enhanced, not overshadowed, by AI. Let us remember that the true power of AI lies not in its algorithms, not in its processing speed, not in its data, but in the hands, hearts, and minds of the humans who create, guide, and use it.

Our task, then, is clear. We must not only imagine our desired future but act to realize it. If we aspire to a world where AI serves as a powerful catalyst for positive change, we must not merely hope for that future. We must shape it, nurture it, and tirelessly work to bring it into being.

It's up to us, all of us, to ensure that AI is the best reflection of who we are and what we can become. Together, we can shape an AI-infused world that is more than just a showcase for technological brilliance, but a testament to human wisdom, resilience, and the enduring power of our shared dreams. Let's ensure that our future is one we can all be proud of, a future that celebrates our humanity even as it amplifies our capabilities.

It's up to us. Let's write a future we'd want to live in.

ABOUT THE AUTHOR

Cara Cusack is a multifaceted author, IT Business Leader, mother, grandmother, and small-scale farmer. Born and raised in Texas, she now calls the beautiful landscapes of Washington State home. With an impressive 25-year career in information technology, Cara's wealth of knowledge is as broad as the landscapes she has traversed, from the green fields of Ireland to the coastal beauty of Malta and the rich jungles of Costa Rica.

While her career initially revolved around the dynamic field of IT, Cara's talents and passions have always stretched beyond the professional realm. She has always found joy in putting pen to paper, but it was a deep-seated belief in freedom of speech that transformed this hobby into a calling. In response to disturbing trends of book bans in schools and public libraries, Cara became determined to share her own voice and began to publish her writings.

Cara's repertoire of work is diverse, ranging from engaging children's stories to compelling fiction and non-fiction for adults. Her belief in diversity, inclusivity, and freedom of expression is often reflected in her work, though she also delights in creating purely fun, imaginative tales. The minds of her children and grandchildren serve as a constant source of inspiration, leading to a medley of stories that are as brilliant and creative as the young minds that helped spark them.

Whether she's penning an insightful piece of non-fiction or spinning a whimsical tale for children, Cara is driven by a love of literature and a commitment to ensuring the freedom and diversity of voices in the literary world. Her array of life experiences, coupled with her professional expertise, imbue her writing with a unique authenticity, making her a celebrated author and a beacon of freedom in literature.

Learn more at CaraCusackBooks.com

ABOUT THE CO-AUTHOR

Martin Cusack is an experienced IT leader and consultant with a diverse background in information technology. With extensive experience in cloud technologies, solutions architecture, and network management, he has successfully designed, analyzed, and implemented enterprise systems for a wide range of organizations.

Martin's expertise lies in his ability to bridge the gap between technical complexities and business objectives. His strategic mindset and analytical skills enable him to deliver comprehensive solutions that optimize resources and drive digital transformation. He has managed large-scale network budgets and implemented network hardware and software to ensure efficient and reliable infrastructure.

Driven by a deep passion for mathematics, AI, and machine learning, Martin is always at the forefront of the latest advancements in these fields. He combines his practical experience with theoretical knowledge to co-author his first book, providing valuable insights and practical guidance for AI and machine learning enthusiasts.

Martin's dedication to continuous learning and his ability to translate complex concepts into actionable strategies make him a trusted advisor, mentor, and thought leader shaping the future of IT.